P9-APU-697

UNEASY NEIGHBOURS
Conflicts That Defined Canada

By Bill Twatio

ESPRIT DE CORPS BOOKS
OTTAWA, CANADA

ABOUT THE AUTHOR

Bill Twatio, a native of Kirkland Lake, Ont., studied at the University of Ottawa, Carleton University, and the University of Toronto. A former public servant and university lecturer, he served with the Algonquin Regiment.

He is a frequent contributor to newspapers and magazines in Canada and the United States on military affairs and social and economic development issues in the Third World.

Bill Twatio has been Associate Editor of *Esprit de Corps* magazine since 1992 and Senior Editor since 2001. He was also the Senior Editor of the two-volume reference set *Canada at War and Peace, II: A Millennium of Military Heritage.*

Copyright © 2005 by Bill Twatio

All rights reserved. No part of this work covered by the copyrights hereon may be reproduced or used in any form or by any means – graphic, electronic or mechanical, including photocopying, recording, taping or information storage and retrieval systems – without the prior written permission of the publisher, or, in the case of photocopying or other reprographic copying, a license from the Canadian Copyright Licensing Agency.

1ST PRINTING – NOVEMBER 2005

LIBRARY AND ARCHIVES OF CANADA CATALOGUING IN PUBLICATION
Twatio, Bill 1944 -
Uneasy neighbours : conflicts that defined Canada / Bill Twatio

ISBN 1-895896-32-0
1. Canada--History, Military--19th century.
2. Canada--History, Military--18th century.
I. Title.

FC226.T824 2005   971   C2005-906608-3

Printed and bound in Canada
Esprit de Corps Books
1066 Somerset Street West, Suite 204
Ottawa, Ontario, K1Y 4T3
1-800-361-2791
www.espritdecorps.ca / espritdecorp@idirect.com

From outside Canada
Tel: (613) 725-5060 / Fax: (613) 725-1019

UNEASY NEIGHBOURS
Conflicts That Defined Canada

By Bill Twatio

esprit de corps

ESPRIT DE CORPS BOOKS
OTTAWA, CANADA

ACKNOWLEDGEMENTS

Misconceptions about the military history of Canada are compounded by the almost complete neglect of that history in the country's schools. There is a cherished national myth that as citizens of a peaceful country, we are unlikely or reluctant warriors. So prevalent is the myth that George F. Stanley, the dean of Canadian military historians subtitled his popular *Canada's Soldiers*, a survey of Canada's military past, "the military history of an unmilitary people." Canadians, even in this, the Year of the Veteran, no longer seem to be aware of how war has shaped the country.

Battles Without Borders is not a comprehensive military history of Canada, rather, it chronicles how war has defined our national identity from the first skirmishes between the Vikings and Dorset peoples, through the rise and fall of New France, the War of 1812, the rebellions in Upper and Lower Canada, to Confederation. How well it succeeds is for the reader to decide.

This book has been very much a collaborative effort. I would like to thank Katherine and Scott Taylor of *Esprit de Corps* for their patience with a sometimes cranky author, and Diana Rank and Darcy Knoll for their unfailing good humour in the face of a monumental editing task. I am particularly grateful to Julie Simoneau, without whose tireless efforts this book would not have been possible.

I am also grateful to Les Peate, who, drawing on his vast knowledge of early warfare and the British army, contributed the piece "To Rule The Waves."

Thank you all.

This book is dedicated to my mother, Rosemary Holland (1914-2004)

CONTENTS

ALSO BY BILL TWATIO:

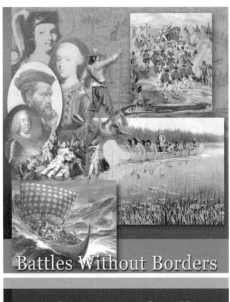

Far from being the "peaceful kingdom" of legend, inhabited by an "umilitary people," Canada has been shaped by war. Not only has war made the very existence of Canada possible, it also shaped our myths and memories, and defined our national identiry.

In *Battles Without Borders*, Bill Twatio chronicles the military history of Canada from the first skirmishes between the Dorset peoples and the Vikings, through to the final fall of New France. *Battles Without Borders* describes how our country was forged in fire.

Other titles published by Esprit de Corps Books:

The War That Wasn't tells the stories of the Canadians and their allies who served during the Korean War.

From Baddeck to the Yalu brings to life the personal histories of the Canadian airmen who flew in the Great War, World War II and Korea.

For more information on these and other Esprit de Corps books, please call 1-800-361-2791 or visit www.espritdecorps.ca.

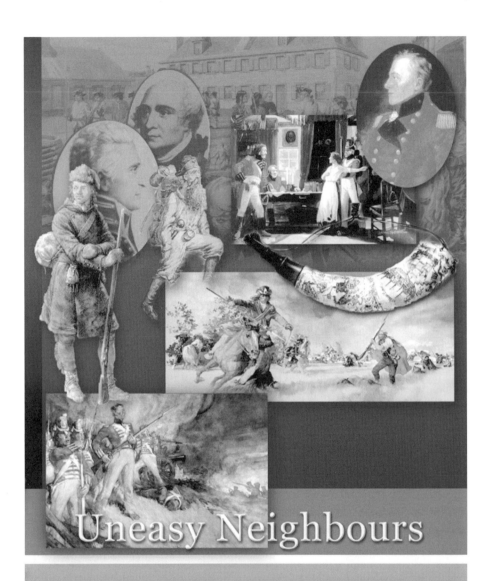

Uneasy Neighbours

Conflicts that defined Canada

BILL TWATIO

✌ A SMALL PEOPLE

The fall of New France was just a prelude to a greater struggle – the American Revolution.

MEETING IN PHILADELPHIA in October 1774, the Continental Congress wrote a manifesto to the people of Canada that was copied in newspapers in Montreal and Quebec. In it, they urged Canadiens to "take a noble chance for emerging from a humiliating subjection under Governors, Intendents, and Military Tyrants" and live as free men, independent of their new masters in London. "You are a small people, compared to those who with open arms invite you into a fellowship," the manifesto declared. "A moment's reflection should convince you which will be most for your interest and happiness, to have all the rest of North America your unalterable friends, or your inveterate enemies."

François Baby, a veteran of the Plains of Abraham and a captain of the militia, noted that the Americans "are preaching rebellion everywhere, urging the pillaging and arrest of the small number of zealous servants of the

RIGHT: *Benjamin Franklin designed this rattlesnake cartoon to urge the British North American colonies to fight in the Seven Years War, which the American refer to as the French and Indian War. The image was revived when the Revolution began. (THE GRANGER COLLECTION)*

OPPOSITE PAGE: *Quebec in the mid-18th century, viewed from across the St. Lawrence. In 1755, the city would once again come under attack. (NAC)*

King, forcing the 'officiers du Roi' to read the proclamations of the rebels from the church doorsteps. They have raised Holy Hell." His sister, Thérèse, a widow with five children, informed him by letter of the situation in Montreal. "You have certainly heard that the 'Bostonnais' (Americans) are giving us quite a fright," she wrote. "You cannot imagine the terror that has overtaken us all – women and men. Many people are getting ready to leave altogether. I am saddened by all of this but then again it does make me laugh to see how some cowards can no longer hide their fear."

After reading the manifesto with its flattery ("exerting the natural sagacity of Frenchmen to consider the matter"), seductions and threats, most Canadiens chose not to endorse either side in the coming struggle between England and America. To them, the American Revolution was nothing more than an argument among Englishmen – "les Bostonnais et les autres." Despite a "mandement" from the Bishop of Quebec proclaiming "the unavoidable duty of defending your country and your King with all the strength you possess," Governor Guy Carleton's summons to the militia brought little response in the Quebec region and angry resistance around Montreal. At least one loyal seigneur was beaten and another driven from his village. Among the Canadiens, the most forceful sentiment was to be left in peace.

Britain had acquired Canada through the fortunes of war. By the Treaty of Paris, signed in 1763, France lost all of New France including Île Royale (Cape Breton Island), Île St. Jean (Prince Edward Island), Newfoundland (except for some ill-defined fishing rights) and the islands of St. Pierre and Miquelon, and its vast territories in the west. France also lost Louisiana, which had been ceded to Spain the year before to prevent it falling into British hands. A Royal Proclamation declared the interior of the continent to be native land. "We do hereby strictly forbid on Pain of our Displeasure," it stated, "all our loving Subjects from making any Purchases or Settlement, whatever, or taking any possession of any of the lands above reserved, without our especial leave and License." The proclamation led to a temporary peace with the western Indian tribes, but caused great resentment in the expansionist Thirteen Colonies. It also antagonized a large number of prominent men, among them George Washington and his fellow investors in the Ohio Company.

The French empire in North America had crumbled, and in its place was a British domain stretching from Hudson Bay to Florida and from the Atlantic seaboard to the Mississippi, anchored on a new colony along the St. Lawrence which the British called Quebec. Much of this huge swath of territory would soon be lost to an emerging United States.

For the people of New France, the change had been monumental, in that they now had new rulers and legally ceased to be French. Still, the change does not seem to have been intolerable to most of the population. The Acadians did suffer a second deportation to clear Prince Edward Island for British settlement, but no attempt was made to disperse the vastly more numerous population on the St. Lawrence. Nor did many people voluntarily return to France rather than take their chances under British rule. Less than three percent returned to the mother country. Those that remained were advised by the Church to pledge loyalty to their new masters, rendering them "what we owed the French when they ruled."

The new governor, James Murray, a veteran of Louisbourg, the Plains of Abraham, and the Battle of Ste-Foy, governed with the assistance of an appointed council, consisting primarily of seigneurs and Catholic clergy. Appropriately, as he oversaw 65,000 French-speaking Catholics, whom he liked, and a swarm of newly arrived English-speaking Protestant merchants, whom he despised. "All have their fortunes to make and I hear few of them are solicitous about the means where the end can be obtained," he wrote. "In general, they are the most immoral collection of men I ever saw."

The most prominent merchant, who Murray described as a "Licentious Fanatick," was Thomas Walker, a native of Boston who arrived in Montreal in the wake of Amherst's armies. Walker, a cantankerous man, insisted that the colony be governed in "the British way," with an elected legislative assembly, which would not allow Catholics to vote or to sit on juries. Murray disagreed. "As there are but 200 Protestant subjects in the province," he said, "the greatest part of which are disbanded soldiers of little Property and mean Capacity, it is thought unjust to exclude the new Roman Catholic subjects to sit upon Juries." Murray knew that he could not govern without the cooperation of the French-speaking majority.

The relationship between Walker and the authorities degenerated into violence. On December 6, 1764, Walker was attacked by a group of masked men – probably soldiers – who beat him until he was "black as a hat" and cut off his right ear. The incident caused an uproar. Although no one was convicted for the attack, it led to Murray's recall to London and his dismissal as governor. Unrepentant, he expressed his pride "in having been accused of warmth and firmness in protecting the King's Canadian Subjects and of doing the utmost in my power to gain to my Royal Master the affection of that brave hardy people, whose Emigration, if it ever shall happen, will be an irreparable Loss to this Empire."

Murray's successor was Guy Carleton, a 42-year-old brigadier-general, who had served as Wolfe's quartermaster and was badly wounded on the Plains of Abraham. Carleton shared Murray's sensibilities, arguing that the imposition of English law on a French and Catholic colony was "barbaric," as well as self-defeating. In office, he nominated twelve Canadian seigneurs to his council, nine of whom had been awarded the Croix de Saint Louis for fighting the British in the Seven Years War.

In 1770, Carleton returned to London to steer the Quebec Act through the House of Commons. It took him four years, but the Act, once passed, conformed to his vision of Canada. Canadiens were guaranteed religious rights and the right to hold public office, French civil law and the seigneurial system of land ownership were upheld, and a legislative council was established. A special oath of loyalty enabled French Canadians to serve on the council – a privilege denied Catholics in Britain.

The Montreal merchants were furious and petitioned the British government, but to no avail. The Act was unpopular in Britain as well. Lord Cavendish warned, "I should think material not to give them (the French), directly their own law again; it keeps up that perpetual dependence upon their ancient laws and customs, which will ever make them a distinct people." When King George III came to Parliament to sign the bill into law, he drove through angry mobs shouting, "No Popery!"

The American colonies saw the Quebec Act as a betrayal. The recognition of French and Catholic rights and the accompanying Royal Proclamation prohibiting settlement west of the Ohio were among the so-called "intolerable acts" that sparked the American Revolution. The American colonists, whose numbers had grown to about 2.2 million – compared to about 85,000 in Canada – coveted this land as a "natural" expansion of their territories. "The finger of God points out a mighty Empire to our sons," a New York newspaper declared. "The Savages of the wilderness were never expelled to make room in this, the best part of the continent, for idolaters and slaves."

Benjamin Franklin met with George Washington, Alexander Hamilton, and other leaders of the American colonies to protest the Quebec Act and resolved "that the last act of Parliament to establish the Roman Catholic religion and French law in the vast country called Canada is an extremely grave danger for the Protestant religion and for the freedoms and civil law of America; consequently, for the citizens and Christian Protestants, we must take the necessary measures to insure our security."

Less than a year later, the American colonies were in open revolt and Canada was in grave danger.

LEFT: *James Murray, the son of British aristocrats, did all he could as governor of Quebec to preserve the French-Canadian presence, for which he was criticized. "I glory in having been accursed of warmth and firmness in protecting the King's Canadian Subjects and of doing the utmost in my power to gain to my Royal Master the affection of that brave, hardy people, whose emigration, if ever it should happen, will be an irreparable Loss to this Empire." (NATIONAL PORTRAIT GALLERY, LONDON)*

OPPOSITE PAGE: *With fewer than 100 men, Ethan Allen and Benedict Arnold seize Fort Ticonderoga before dawn on May 10, 1775, and take Captain William Delaplace and his wife completely by surprise. (THE GRANGER COLLECTION)*

 REBELS IN RED COATS

Deploring the "Sorrows and Afflictions of our suffering Brethren," Congress invites Canada to join the Revolution, but most Canadians remained indifferent.

ON THE NIGHT OF December 16, 1773, a mob of malcontents disguised as Mohawks marched down to a wharf in Boston harbour where the British ship *Dartmouth* lay at anchor with 300 chests of tea in her hold. In protest against a tax on tea imposed upon the colonies without their consent, the saboteurs smashed the chests with their tomahawks and hurled the contents overboard. It was the latest in a series of disturbances that would provoke the war that was to win the Americans their independence; a war which would threaten the very existence of Canada.

In command of British troops in Canada was an experienced 50-year-old Irish officer, Major General Guy Carleton, the Governor of Quebec. Carleton had fought under Wolfe on the Plains of Abraham where he had been badly wounded. He had made a name for himself as one of the bravest and most talented officers in the army and had been appointed acting governor in 1767. Much respected by the French for his endorsement of the Quebec

Act, which allowed Catholics to practise their religion and re-established the authority of French civil law in Canada, he was regarded with suspicion and widespread dislike by English-speaking merchants in Montreal.

Fearing that the Quebec Act would surround the fledgling United States with "a Nation of Papists and Slaves," the Continental Congress established a Committee of Correspondence to enlist support in Canada. Deploring "the Sorrows and Afflictions of our suffering Brethren," Congress invited them to join the cause. The Americans had some support as disgruntled citizens in Montreal had defaced a bust of George III in a public square, suspending a rosary made of potatoes around the royal neck with a wooden cross bearing the words: "Voilà le Pape du Canada et le Sot Anglais." But most remained indifferent. Rural Canadians, known as *habitants* or *Canadiens* to the British, also ignored the call of "les Bostonnais." In the summer of 1775, entreaties gave way to preparations for invasion.

Carleton had frequently complained of the weakness of the garrisons in Canada and the reluctance of successive administrations to reinforce them. "There are not 600 Rank and File fit for Duty upon the whole Extent of this great River," he reported to London. "Not an armed Vessel or Place of Strength and the ancient Provincial Force is enervated and broke to pieces." When he learned that 2000 American troops were on the march, he feared that he would be unable to resist them.

The American forces, approaching in two columns, were led by Benedict Arnold who had been ordered by General George Washington to take Quebec and by Richard Montgomery, a former officer in the British Army who was charged with taking Montreal and then joining Arnold for the attack on Quebec. Carleton was in a very weak position with his regulars scattered. He had dispatched 800 infantry to General Thomas Gage in Boston the year before and he would have to face the invaders with what he perceived to be an unreliable militia. Moreover, he could not expect reinforcements in the immediate future.

Ticonderoga at the head of Lake Champlain fell to Ethan Allen and his Green Mountain Boys in May, with Allen demanding the surrender of the fortress "in the name of the Great Jehovah and the Continental Congress." Chambly and Fort St. Jean on the Richelieu fell to Montgomery. Carleton, repulsed when he marched south with a pitifully small force, found it neces-

RIGHT: On December 31, 1775, General Richard Montgomery and his men attacked Quebec in a raging blizzard. (NEW YORK PUBLIC LIBRARY)

sary to retreat to Montreal, a captured Ethan Allen in tow, resplendent in deerskins. Montreal was abandoned in November. The rag-tag Americans marched through the Récollet gate to eagerly seize stockpiles of warm, red British tunics and to so wantonly plunder the town that an officer claimed that Carleton would soon have as many Canadian volunteers anxious to fight the rebels as he could possibly desire. Carleton himself was almost captured, but escaped in a whaleboat disguised as a fisherman. He arrived in Quebec a week later and immediately set about preparing its defences.

Benedict Arnold and his 1000 men faced an appalling task when they set off in September 1774 to march up the Kennebec and Chaudière Rivers through the forests of Maine. For three weeks they struggled through mile after mile of wilderness and swamp, their uniforms torn to shreds and their provisions running so low that they were forced to eat their dogs. Some died of exhaustion and 300 deserted. A survivor recalled:

"It rained heavily and turned to a snowstorm, and the snow fell knee-deep. Our company was obliged to kill a dog and eat it for breakfast, and in the course of that day I killed an owl, and two of my messmates and myself shared in the repast. The day following, we waded a river 30 rods wide... Next day started, and I was taken sick of a kind of camp distemper. I could not walk far in a day... I became so feeble that myself and two more hired a Frenchman to carry us at our expense for 13 miles... We then went on, all very much enfeebled by reason of sickness and hardship, for four or five days until we reached Quebec."

When Arnold arrived at Quebec he had fewer than 600 men left. After leading an abortive sortie against the town, he dug in at Pointe-aux-Trembles to wait for Montgomery. He arrived on December 3, with no more than 300 men and a few gunners. Advancing together, they occupied the suburbs, their men thankful for any shelter from the wind. It was bitterly cold now and the ground was frozen hard. Attempts to dig siege lines proved futile, the troops contenting themselves with piling up banks of snow and ice before "hundreds of gaping citizens and soldiers" standing on the walls. They had no siege artillery and a bombardment by field guns did little damage. Nor had they any means of blockading the river. As many of their men had enlisted only until the end of the year and were anxious to return home, Arnold and Montgomery were determined to attempt an assault as soon as possible.

At two o'clock New Year's Eve morning, in a blinding snowstorm, the Americans attacked. Alerted to their posts by the ringing of church bells, the garrison opened up a heavy fire with musket and grapeshot. Running forward with his men, Montgomery was shot in the face and died in the arms of a young lieutenant. In Lower Town, Arnold was wounded in the leg charging a barricade below the ramparts and had to be carried away on a scaling ladder. Leaving 75 dead and 426 prisoners behind, his men scurried across the frozen St. Charles River and settled down for a long siege.

The Americans were still before Quebec at dawn on May 6, when a salute from the frigate *Surprise* rounding Île d'Orléans awoke the town to the realization that relief was at hand. The *Isis*, the sloop *Martin*, and five transports followed in her wake. "The news soon reached every pillow in town," a witness said, "and people half dress'd ran down to the Grand Battery to feast their eyes." Troops were landed and without delay were joined by regulars and militia from the garrison. With Carleton in command, the force marched out of the city to St. Roch as the Americans took to their heels leaving guns, mortars, field pieces and muskets behind. Carleton did not force a battle. He was content to let his men enjoy the breakfast the Americans had prepared for themselves but had no opportunity to eat.

OPPOSITE PAGE: *General Richard Montgomery is mortally wounded in Lower Town during the failed assault on Quebec.* (PAINTING BY ALONYS CHAPPEL, CHICAGO HISTORICAL SOCIETY)

🎺 THE WOODEN HORSE

One challenge is answered by another as two sides prepare to square off on the ramparts of Quebec.

DAYS BEFORE HIS ILL-FATED attack on Quebec, General Richard Montgomery issued general orders to his troops promising them loot when the city fell. The orders included the following: "The General is confident that a vigorous and spirited attack must be attended with success. The troops shall have the personal effects of the Governor, garrison, and of such as have been acting in misleading the inhabitants and distressing the friends of liberty to be equally divided among them." Hoping to rattle the garrison, he had an Indian attach the order to an arrow and shoot it over the walls.

Carleton waged his own brand of psychological warfare. While inspecting the walls of the city, he noticed an elevated sentry box on the ramparts of Cape Diamond. Borrowing a large wooden rocking horse from his son's nursery, he secured it to a board facing the box which he filled with hay and placed a sign around its neck announcing: "Je ne rendrai point Québec jusqu'à ce que le cheval ait mangé le foin!" (I shall not surrender Quebec until the horse has eaten the hay!) His challenge was all over the city within hours and men, women, and children climbed Cape Diamond to view "Carleton's horse."

The horse went hungry.

BOTTOM: *Rushing to meet Benedict Arnold's units for a surprise attack on Quebec City on New Year's Eve, 1775, General Richard Montgomery reels backward as he is mortally wounded, still holding his sword.* (NATIONAL GEOGRAPHIC SOCIETY)

LEFT AND BELOW: *The hilt of the sword used by Montgomery and his beautifully carved powder horn.* (ROYAL ONTARIO MUSEUM)

OPPOSITE PAGE: *On October 10, 1776, Carleton's ships met Benedict Arnold's in Valcour Bay on Lake Champlain.* (MARINERS' MUSEUM)

❧ CARLETON'S BATTLE OF LAKE CHAMPLAIN

Guy Carleton and Benedict Arnold transform themselves into sailors and fight for control of Lake Champlain.

LANDLUBBER BUT NO MEAN naval strategist, Guy Carleton realized that he must take Ticonderoga and regain control of Lake Champlain to forestall another American invasion of Canada. And so, in the summer of 1776, he transformed himself into a sailor and began to build a fleet.

At St. Jean on the Richelieu, the woods rang to the sound of hammers and saws as soldiers and sailors, artificers and carpenters worked in the summer heat under the supervision of Captain Thomas Pringle, Carleton's naval adviser. At the far end of the Lake, the Americans, under Benedict Arnold, another inveterate landlubber, were equally busy building their own fleet.

By October 1776, Carleton was ready to move. On October 9, he set sail with the spanking new schooners *Inflexible, Maria,* and *Carleton* mounting 18, 14 and 12 guns respectively, followed by the gun ketch *Thunderer*, the *Loyal Convert*, 12-gun boats and 50 flat-bottomed bateaux. At his end of the lake, Arnold set out with the refloated schooner *Royal Savage*, the *Revenge*, the *Philadelphia*, the cutters *Lee* and *Enterprise*, and three row galleys well armed with ten to 16 guns each. Anchoring off Valcour Island, he drew his ships into line and waited for the British.

On the morning of October 10, the *Carleton* caught the *Royal Savage* off the north end of the island. Run aground by her green and inexperienced crew, she was burned by a British boarding party. Meanwhile, the gunboats, using their oars, closed with Arnold's line. The ensuing battle raged for hours, directed by Pringle aboard the *Maria* with Carleton at his side. The *Philadelphia* was sunk and a British gunboat blew up when a shot hit her magazine. A large contingent of Indians who had accompanied Carleton's fleet in their canoes landed on the island and harassed the American crews with long range musket fire. Out of ammunition, the gunboats fell back to seek the protection of the larger vessels.

That night Arnold managed to sail his battered flotilla through Carleton's line. Setting off in pursuit, Carleton forced the *Washington* and *New Jersey* to strike their colours and ran *Lee* aground. Pounded by heavy British fire, Arnold beached the *Congress* and set her ablaze before making off into the woods near Chimney Point. Narrowly escaping an Indian ambush, he reached Crown Point the following day. His crews were rounded up by the British, given a lecture by Carleton who praised them for their bravery, and were then released and sent home on condition that they not serve again until formally exchanged.

Carleton returned to Quebec at the beginning of November and sent his men into winter quarters. On New Year's Eve, back in his general's uniform, he gave a dinner for 60 guests followed by a public fête and a grand ball, 12 months to the day since he had hurled back Montgomery and Arnold's invasion.

OPPOSITE PAGE: *Sir Guy Carleton, 1st Baron Dorchester (1724-1808). An Irish-born British army officer, Carleton swerved as governor of Quebec from 1768-78 and again between 1785-95. As commander-in-chief of British North America, he opposed the Constitutional Act of 1791 dividing Quebec into Upper and Lower Canada.* (NAC)

 SIR GUY CARLETON

CANADA HAS RARELY HAD such a friend. Soldier and statesman, an honest man in a dishonest age, Guy Carleton dominated the first 30 years of Canada's existence under British rule and secured its future.

As a soldier, he successfully defended the citadel of Quebec in 1775 and drove the invaders from Canadian soil. Had he failed, Canada might well have become the 14th state in the emerging United States of America. Succeeding Cornwallis as commander-in-chief of all British forces in North America following the surrender at Yorktown, he oversaw the peaceful withdrawal of British forces spread along the Atlantic seaboard and the transportation of some 30,000 Loyalists to Nova Scotia.

As a statesman, he conceived and formulated the Quebec Act, one of the key documents in Canadian history, which guaranteed the inhabitants of Quebec their language, their civil law, their religion, and the right to hold public office. A unique piece of legislation for its time, it was the first tentative step in the building of the second British Empire and the first step toward the creation of what came to be known as the Commonwealth. He was also the prophet of a Canadian federation.

Although trained to be a soldier, he was a humane man who detested war. He considered American rebels deluded Englishmen, and to the consternation of the British government insisted on releasing and returning prisoners of war to their homes. Wounded four times in the course of his military career, he was blessed with a magnificent constitution. He made the dangerous Atlantic crossing 14 times and, on his last voyage shortly after his 72nd birthday, he was shipwrecked but came through unscathed. At the age of 47, he married a girl of 18 who he scarcely knew. Devoted to him, she bore him 11 children.

He stood six feet tall and walked with an erect military posture. His portraits show a remarkable resemblance to George Washington. Both men had a stern, serious, aloof manner and it is hard to imagine them laughing. Wolfe referred to the "grave Carleton," but added, "One should not be repelled by his cold manners as he is a perfect gentleman and one of the best officers in the service." He would listen to anyone, talk to anyone. It was reported that when a Canadien had a complaint, the common expression was: "Je vais le dire au Général Carleton." (I shall tell it to General Carleton.)

His biographer, Sir Charles Lucas, said of him: "Of Carleton's merits as a soldier there can be no question. No one ever displayed more firmness and courage at a time of crisis, made more of small resources, or showed more self-restraint. But he was more than a good military man, he was a statesman of high order, and, had he been given a free hand and supreme control of the British forces and policy in America, he might well have kept the American colonies as he kept Quebec ... Above all, he had a character above and beyond intrigue."

Guy Carleton died in his 84th year at Stubbing, in Berkshire. He is buried in the vault of Nately Scures, a tiny, 12th century chapel overlooking his Greywell Hill estate.

OPPOSITE PAGE: *Major General Sir John Burgoyne, English general and playwright, he is largely remembered for capitulating to the Americans at Saratoga in 1777 while commanding British forces in Canada.* (THE FRICK COLLECTION, NEW YORK)

❧ THE ROAD TO SARATOGA

Contemptuous of the "Yankee Rabble,"
'Gentleman Johnny' Burgoyne moves
south with thousands of troops and a bold
plan to end the rebellion.

AFTER 40 DAYS AT SEA aboard the frigate *Apollo*, John Burgoyne stepped ashore at Quebec in a well-tailored uniform in May 1777 to assume command of His Majesty's troops in Canada. Although dismayed by having been superseded by Sir Guy Carleton, an officer who had recently been his subordinate and who remained in his post as governor, Burgoyne nonetheless offered all the assistance he could.

The previous summer Carleton had driven the Americans out of the St. Lawrence Valley, gained naval command of Lake Champlain, and laid siege to Fort Ticonderoga. As the season advanced and with an eye to his supply lines, he withdrew in November to send his army into winter quarters. Ever cautious, he did not share Burgoyne's contempt for the "Yankee rabble."

Poet and playwright, dandy and bon vivant, Burgoyne had been nick-

Lieutenant General John Burgoyne addresses his Indian allies in the summer of 1777. Illustration by H. Warren, engraved by J.C. Armytage. (NAC/C-17514)

named "Gentleman Johnny" by his adoring troops. An adroit politician as well, he had sold the cabinet in London on a daring plan for ending the rebellion. Moving out of Canada down the Richelieu and Lake Champlain to the Hudson River to link up with troops sweeping through the Adirondacks and coming upriver from New York, he would split the American colonies in two. If he had any doubts about the likely success of his plan, they were not evident in his florid General Orders to his army:

"We embark tomorrow to approach the Enemy. We are to contend for the King and the Constitution of Great Britain, to vindicate the Law and relieve the Oppressed, a cause in which we all feel equal Excitement. The Services required on this particular Expedition are critical and conspicuous. During our progress occasions may occur in which neither difficulty, nor labour, nor Life are to be regarded. THIS ARMY MUST NOT RETREAT!"

And on a beautiful spring morning in June, the army set off to the sound of skirling pipes and drums. There were 3700 British regulars; 3000 German mercenaries commanded by Baron Friedrich von Riedesel accompanied by his baroness, Fredericka, their three young children, two maids travelling in a large calash, 650 Canadians, 400 Indians drawn from the Six Nations, loyal Tory auxiliaries led by Philip Skene who was attended by black servants in splendid livery and powdered wigs (Skene, the laird of Scots Bay, lived in a house in which his mother's corpse reposed on a table so that she might still receive the annuity guaranteed her so long as she remained "above ground"), and 600 artillerymen with 138 guns. Burgoyne brought up the rear with 30 carts carrying his uniforms and personal bag-

In an attempt to slow Bourgoyne's advance, Americans employed scorched-earth tactics including burning crops, cutting down trees, and destroying bridges. Here, the wife of General Philip Schuyler burns the family's wheat. (THE GRANGER COLLECTION)

gage, a splendid selection of French wines and his mistress, the wife of a commissary official. When assembled, the expedition stretched out for three miles.

Fort Ticonderoga, lightly guarded and further weakened by quarrels between officers and men, fell to Burgoyne on July 4, the second anniversary of the Declaration of Independence. Forts Anne, Edward, Skenesboro, and Hubbardton were taken a few days later. In less than three weeks the British covered 100 miles, captured the enemy's most important fortresses and took scores of prisoners at a loss of a very small fraction of their force. They had only 40 miles to go before reaching Albany where they could expect news of William Howe's army in the south. Then, Burgoyne's relentless march began to falter.

The weather turned bad. Rain poured down in torrents washing away bridges, and soaking uniforms and stores. The roads became impassible with wagons breaking down in the mud. The Americans, under the able command of General Horatio Gates, who was dismissed by Burgoyne as "that old midwife," adopted a scorched-earth policy, burning crops and herding livestock away. With astonishing vigour, they felled hundreds of trees across the roads." We are obliged to wait for some time in our present position till the roads are cleared," one of Burgoyne's officers wrote. "Every 10 or 12 yards great trees are laid across our path." As well as dragging away trees, the men had to work day and night building bridges and causeways across the creeks and marshes beneath which the roads disappeared with exasperating frequency. Nor could the British expect help from the local

LEFT: *English-born General Horatio Gates approached Congress to obtain command of the American armies. Politically ambitious, he would later scheme to depose George Washington as commander-in-chief.* (INDEPENDENCE NATIONAL HISTORICAL PARK)

OPPOSITE PAGE: *Benedict Arnold leads a charge across Freeman's Farm. Horatio Gates, jealous of Arnold's accomplishments, did not even mention his name in his report on the battle. (AMERICAN HERITAGE)*

population. Already informed that "to give aid and comfort to the enemy would be punished as treason to the United States," they were enraged by the depredations of Burgoyne's Indian allies.

So successful were the American attempts to slow him down that Burgoyne – hampered by his heavy artillery and supply trains – was reduced to marching less than a mile a day. To maintain even the slow momentum of his advance, he soon realized that more baggage animals were essential. On Baron von Riedesel's advice, he decided to stage a raid on Bennington where there were reported to be at least 100 horses besides large supplies of food and ammunition. Bloodily repulsed, the few survivors of the raid staggered back into his lines a week later. "We do not know how many we have killed," a rebel wrote. "Our scouts daily find them dead in the woods. One of our scouts found, the beginning of this week, 26 of the enemy lying dead in the woods. They stank so they could not bury them… The wounded Hessians die three or four a day. They are all in Bennington Meeting House which smells so it is enough to kill anyone in it." Burgoyne lost four cannon, and perhaps as many as 900 soldiers.

A deep sense of apprehension now ran through the British camp, compounded by news that the Adirondack force had been defeated and that Howe had not moved out of New York.

On September 8, General Gates marched 11,000 men to a high plateau near Saratoga known as Bemis Heights. Here and at nearby Freeman's Farm, he dug in and waited for Burgoyne. On the morning of the 17th, exuding a cheerful confidence that infected his staff, Burgoyne attacked. "The conflict was dreadful," a soldier recalled. "For four hours a constant fire was

kept up… Men, and particularly officers dropped every moment on each side." British regiments made one bayonet charge after another but were driven back. Benedict Arnold, still limping from the wound he received at Quebec, was the man of the hour. "Nothing could exceed the bravery of Arnold on this day," one of his officers recalled. "He seemed the very genius of war. Infuriated by the conflict and knowing he was meeting the brunt of the battle, he seemed inspired with the fury of the demon." At nightfall, having lost a third of their strength, the British retreated into Saratoga. Surrounded, Burgoyne surrendered on October 17.

His once proud army began its last march the following day as an American military band played *Yankee Doodle Dandy*, a British army song of the Seven Years War. "To be sure, the sight was truly astonishing," Saratoga resident Hanna Winthrop wrote. "I have never had the least idea that the Creator produced such a sordid set of creatures in human figure – poor, dirty, emaciated men, great numbers of women, who seemed to be the beasts of burden, having a bushel basket on their back, by which they were bent double; the contents seemed to be pots and kettles, various sorts of furniture, children peeping through gridirons and other utensils, some very young infants who were born on the road, the women's bare feet, clothed in dirty rags; such effluvia filled the air while they were passing that I was apprehensive of being contaminated by them."

Winthrop noted that Burgoyne, in an immaculate uniform, rode at the head of this pitiful procession.

❧ THE BARONESS' CHRISTMAS TREE

Amidst the horror and hardship of war in the wilderness, a German aristocrat won the affection of the rank and file.

KNOWN TO HER FAMILY as *Fritschen*, her dark blue eyes were full of laughter and her smile was pure delight. At 17, the German artist Tischbein, painted her as "Spring" with her hair pinned up in a pompadour crowned with flowers. In time she would be known as *The Baroness, Lady Fritz,* or *Mrs. General,* the indomitable wife of Friedrich Adolph von Riedesel, commander of the Duke of Brunswick's mercenaries in America. She would ride into the wilderness with her husband and write a first-hand account of her adventures in America during the Revolutionary War. When published, an engraver would reproduce the Tischbein portrait as a frontispiece, but his sentimental re-drawing would only faintly resemble the gay young girl of the original or the handsome, mature woman painted in later life.

Camp followers were no strangers to 18th century armies. However, few were as resourceful as the Baroness, who, with her three young daughters,

RIGHT: *The custom of decorating Christmas trees dates back to 1604 in Strasbourg.* (ILLUSTRATED LONDON NEWS)

OPPOSITE PAGE: *Baroness Frederika von Riedesel.* (ENGRAVING BY J.C. BUTTRE AFTER TISCHBEIN PAINTING, NEW YORK PUBLIC LIBRARY)

accompanied her husband on John Burgoyne's ill-fated march to Saratoga in the summer of 1777 after enduring a 13-month journey to Canada, in the course of which she had been swindled by a confidence man, left almost destitute by the romantic aspirations of a companion, was mistaken for a French prostitute by a mob of sailors, and befriended by King George III.

On New Year's Day 1777, the Baroness was invited to the Court of St. James. "I found the palace very ugly and furnished in an old-fashioned style," she wrote. The King chatted confidently about America. The Queen was also friendly and discussed her coming trip. "I admire your courage," she told the Baroness, "for that is a great undertaking, and especially difficult with three children."

No admirer of "Gentleman Johnny" Burgoyne, whom she considered as arrogant as he was incompetent, the Baroness noted that "it was only too true that he likes to make himself easy, and that he spent half his nights in singing and drinking, and diverting himself with his mistress who was as fond of champagne as himself."

Travelling in a carriage with her daughters, the Baroness recalled: "The country was magnificent, but all the people had gone to strengthen the American army... Every inhabitant is a born soldier and a good marksman; in addition, the thought of fighting for freedom made them braver than ever."

As the weather turned bad and the march slowed down, Friedrich von Riedesel's unhappy dragoons, horseless and awkward on foot as they slogged along in their heavy Brunswick jack-boots, became laughingstocks. The laughter, however, did not extend to the Baroness who, in a play on her name, was known to the British and Canadian rank and file as "Red'azel" with the H dropped off in cockney-fashion – and it would soon become a term of admiration and affection. As for the Germans, she was their Baroness – symbolic of everything good and beautiful that they longed for when they thought of home.

Good in good times and even better in bad, the Baroness cared for the sick and wounded and comforted the dying. Forced to take shelter in a basement in besieged Saratoga, she wrote: "On the following morning the cannonade again began, but from a different side. I advised all to go out of the cellar for a little while, during which time I would have it cleaned as otherwise we would all be sick. They followed my suggestion, and I at once set many hands to work, which was in the highest degree necessary, for the women and children, being afraid to venture forth, had soiled the whole cellar. I had just given the cellar a good sweeping and had fumigated by sprinkling vinegar on burning coals and each one had found his place prepared for him, when a fresh and terrible cannonade threw us all once more into alarm. Many persons, who had no right to come in, threw themselves against the door. My children were already under the cellar steps and we would all have been crushed if God had not given me strength enough to place myself before the door and with extended arms prevent all from coming in. Eleven cannon balls went through the house and we could plainly hear them rolling on the floor over our heads. One poor soldier, whose leg they were about to amputate, having been laid upon a table for this purpose, had the other leg taken off by another cannon ball in the very middle of the operation. I was more dead than alive, though not so much on account of my own danger for that which enveloped my husband, who, however, frequently sent to see how I was getting along, and to tell me he was still safe. We had no water because the enemy shot every man in the head who went near the river… In this horrible situation we remained for almost a week."

With the surrender of Saratoga, the Baroness was escorted into the American lines. When she arrived at General Horatio Gate's headquarters, the general lifted her children into his arms, kissed them and took the family to his own tent where his cook gave them a meal. He then returned to a parley with Burgoyne. "General Gates and his principal guests were drinking rum and water from the only two available glasses," the Baroness noted. "Burgoyne was asked to propose a toast. He stood, and with his glass in hand announced, 'George Washington!' They drank the toast and waited for General Gates to respond. He rose and said, 'King George III!'"

The Baroness and her children then marched into captivity along with remnants of Burgoyne's army. A witness recalled their passing: "I have never had the least idea that the Creator produced such a sordid set of creatures in human figure: poor, dirty, emaciated men, great numbers of women in bare feet, clothed in dirty rags, children and some very young infants. Such effluvia filled the air that I was apprehensive of being contaminated by them."

Reunited with her husband, the Baroness spent her last years in Canada at Sorel, Quebec, in a house specially built for her by the governor of Quebec, Sir Frederick Haldimand, which overlooked the Richelieu River. On Christmas Day, 1781, she sat down to dinner with her family and officers of the garrison. They had turkey and plum pudding, she noted in her diary, which was "an English custom." In turn, she introduced her guests to an old German custom. At the centre of her dining room stood a large evergreen decorated with candles and white ribbons – the first Christmas tree ever seen in Canada.

The von Riedesels returned to their native Brunswick in 1783 with many fond memories of Canada – and a baby girl named Amerika.

After Burgoyne's surrender at Saratoga, American General Horatio Gates invited him to refreshments in his tent. (THE GRANGER COLLECTION).

❧ THE LOYALISTS

Reviled and reduced to poverty, tens of thousands reject the new Republic.

"*I CLIMBED THE TOP* of Chipman's Hill," the grandmother of Sir Leonard Tilley, a Father of Confederation, recalled, "and watched the sails disappearing in the distance, and such a feeling of loneliness came over me that, although I had not shed a tear through all the war, I sat down on the damp moss with my baby on my lap and cried."

She had reason to cry. In May 1783, she and 3000 Loyalists came ashore from seven ships anchored off the mouth of the Saint John River. Another 11,000 would land before the end of the year. They had been promised a land of plenty by colonial officials who spoke of "a fine river accessible in all seasons" and the many settlers "who get their living easily." Thirteen Loyalist regiments had accepted the claims as true. Now, as winter approached, they found themselves without land or provisions. In Saint John, they huddled in tents. "We pitched our tents in the shelter of the woods and tried to cover them with spruce boughs," one woman said. "We had no floors but

RIGHT: Many Loyalists were forced to flee in the face of persecution from their neighbours, leaving their land and most of their possessions behind. (PAINTING BY HOWARD PYLE, DELAWARE ART MUSEUM)

OPPOSITE PAGE: *The first of the Loyalist refugees arrive in Saint John, New Brunswick in 1783. (PAINTING BY ADAM SHERRIFF SCOTT, NEW BRUNSWICK MUSEUM)*

the ground and snow drifted in. Many women and children and some of the men died."

In Halifax, Loyalists were crowded into sheds, stores and warehouses. Exiles from the Carolinas ran short of food and died on a hill that would become known as Mount Misery. In Quebec, they were looked upon as unwelcome guests and packed off into the wilderness. Bitter, they began to turn on each other. Nova Scotia was mocked as "Nova Scarcity," the original settlers were denounced as "Bluenoses" and their loyalty to the Crown questioned. The governor, mixing metaphors, condemned them as "a cursed set of dogs" and "people preying on one another like sharks."

Some 35,000 Loyalists settled in the Maritimes; among them were several thousand blacks who had escaped slavery. Retreating north with the British army, their numbers became a hindrance. They were sometimes so desperate that they clung to the sides of boats. "To prevent this dangerous practice, the fingers of some of them were chopped off, and soldiers were posted with cutlasses and bayonets to oblige them to keep at proper distances," a soldier recalled. "Many of them labouring under diseases, forsaken by their new masters, and destitute of the necessities of life, perished in the woods."

To avoid destitution, some black Loyalists sold themselves to merchants for two or years of service, effectively returning to the slavery they had

On the frontier, raiding parties of Loyalists and Iroquois swept down from British bases to spread death and destruction. The massacre in the Wyoming Valley was the worst, where Iroquois warriors took 227 scalps. (CHICAGO HISTORICAL SOCIETY)

escaped. Famine was rampant and crimes of desperation were punished harshly. In Shelbourne, a town blacks built, a black woman received 200 lashes for stealing a shilling. On July 26, 1784, the blacks were driven out of Shelbourne. "Great riot today," the surveyor Benjamin Marston wrote. "The disbanded soldiers have risen against the Free Negroes to drive them out of Town, because they labour cheaper than they do. The soldiers force the Free Negroes to quit the town – pulled down about 20 of their houses."

While many blacks stayed and built a permanent community, almost 1200 black Loyalists, a third of the population, sailed for Africa to establish a colony at Freetown in Sierra Leone.

The Americans who supported the British cause during the Revolution were well acquainted with abuse. Branded as Tories, their homes had been sacked and burned, they were denied the right to vote, to sell land, and to sue debtors. Some were beaten by mobs and some lynched by Patriots, self-styled "Sons of Liberty." The Continental Congress ordered Committees of Public Safety to find, identify, and punish Tories, or Loyalists as they were increasingly known. George Washington suggested that, in simple decency, they should all commit suicide.

As early as 1769, the Patriots set about deliberately trying to terrify opponents. Tar and feathers were their most frightening weapons. A Loyalist would sometimes be approached on a street by a stranger who would slip a small ball of cold tar into his hand. The threat was clear. Regarded more as a joke than punishment, the reality was anything but. A victim was usually stripped to the waist and covered with boiling pine tar and chicken feathers and paraded around on a rail. Removal of the tar was just as painful as its application.

Determined to fight back, many Tories joined Loyalist regiments after Paul Revere's ride and the clashes at Lexington and Concord. It has been estimated that over the course of the American Revolution between 30,000 to 50,000 Loyalist enlisted in 300 commissioned companies. Others organized themselves into armed bands. At first, Loyalist troops lacked uniforms and were often shot at by both sides. To avoid confusion, they were issued green uniforms to distinguish them from red-coated regulars. "Green," wrote Colonel John Graves Simcoe of the Queen's Rangers, "is without comparison the best colour for light troops ...and if it is put on in the spring, by autumn it nearly fades with the leaves, preserving its characteristics of being scarcely discernible at distance." By virtue of their uniforms, the Rangers were particularly useful as skirmishers.

Loyalists were used primarily as raiders and shock troops as they knew the country and could move silently through the forests. The Queen's Rangers, however, distinguished themselves on the field of traditional combat with the British army. At Brandywine, they were ordered to attack American artillery batteries. "The fourth Regiment led the column," Ensign Stephen Jarvis wrote, "and the Rangers followed. The enemy fired upon us with grape shot... As we crossed a creek the water took us up to our breasts and was much stained with blood." But the guns were taken and turned on the enemy.

Along the Niagara frontier, John Butler, a former landowner in the Mohawk Valley, and Joseph Brant recruited the Iroquois to disrupt American forces. By the summer of 1778, they were leading raiding parties up and down the Mohawk and Cherry valleys. Enraged, Congress ordered General John Sullivan to clear the Six Nations out of their historic homeland in the Finger Lakes District of New York. No quarter was to be given. As Sullivan moved north burning crops and villages, the Iroquois fled into the hills, many dying of starvation. In the winter of 1779, the survivors straggled into Canada seeking food and protection.

The Six Nations had effectively been destroyed, but there was concern in Britain that they might rally and seek revenge. To forestall this, the Six

LEFT: *Loyalist refugees were forced to abandon their land and belongings, and endured bitter privation. The state of New York made $3.6 million from selling confiscated Loyalist property.* (THE GRANGER COLLECTION)

OPPOSITE PAGE: *The map indicates the names of the various regiments, and where they settled in the area of the Saint John River.*

Nations were granted Crown lands north of Lake Erie. Brant and 1800 fellowers settled along the Grand River in the fall of 1784. He died in 1807. His last words were: "Have pity on the poor Indians; if you can get any influence with the great, endeavour to do them all the good you can."

For their services, Butler's Rangers received land on the west bank of the Niagara River. Butler settled there and so did Peter Bowman, one of his officers. "My father settled on his land near the fort," his daughter wrote. "He drew an axe and a hoe from the Government... My mother had a cow, a bed, six plates, and three knives... Men, women and children all went to work clearing the land."

The defeat of Burgoyne at Saratoga sent shock waves through the Loyalist troops. Word spread of mistreatment of prisoners. According to one report, "a man half dead with his left eye smashed open by a musket ball was slung on a horse and led around for the amusement of rebel militiamen. Other prisoners were ordered tied in pairs and attached by traced to horses. They were ordered to tramp their way through deep snows to make roads for the rebels to use, while clad only in thin shoes, or actually barefoot."

The activities of Loyalist regiments reduced the fighting strength of Washington's armies. Their efforts, however, were not enough to bring victory. In October 1781, General Charles Cornwallis surrendered at Yorktown

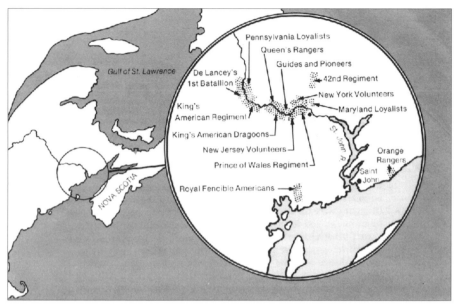

and the American Revolution was over.

"You cannot conceive," a British colonel wrote, "nor can any language describe the distress that all ranks of people here have been thrown into by the Independence of America being acknowledged by Great Britain, and the Loyalists being given up to the mercies of their Enemies." Loyalist regiments were disbanded and each soldier given a choice: return home with three months' pay or be transported to Nova Scotia. Very few went home.

General Sir Guy Carleton assumed responsibility for evacuating Loyalists. Fearing for their safety if they were exposed to "the rage and violence" of the American people, he refused to withdraw British troops from New York until the last ship sailed to the taunts of a popular verse:

"Tories with their brats and wives/Should fly to save their wretched lives."

The Loyalists who took ship were a varied lot. There were lawyers and farmers, carpenters and clergymen, soldiers and slaves, graduates of Harvard and men who could not write their own names. They faced a forbidding, lonely country. "The roughest land I ever saw," said one. Five of every six settled in Nova Scotia which was poorly prepared for a sudden tripling of its population. Colonel Edward Winslow reported people were "crowded into one spot without covering, and totally ignorant where they are eventually to settle." He listened to men "addressing me in a language which almost murdered me as I heard it. 'Sir, we have served all the war, your honour is witness how faithfully. We were promised land… only let us have a spot of our own.'"

Eventually, they began to clear the land on grants that ranged from 100 to 500 acres and, with tools, food and supplies provided by the British, founded communities at Wallace, Parrsboro, St. Stephen and St. Andrews. Along the Saint John River, they demanded a self-governing colony of their own. Accordingly, in August 1784, Nova Scotia was cut off at the Chignecto isthmus and New Brunswick was born.

In Quebec, thousands of Loyalists threatened to swamp the predominately French population. Some settled on government land around Sorel or headed northeast to the Gaspé, Peninsula. In 1784, with the approval of the Indians, Governor Frederick Haldimand threw open the region beyond the Ottawa River and more than 5,000 were loaded aboard scows and transported into the "Western Settlements."

Regiment by regiment, the Loyalists moved west – the King's Royal Regiment, the Loyal Rangers, the King's Rangers. Worn and faded uniforms blended into the forests along the St. Lawrence, at Cataraqui (what is now Kingston), around the Bay of Quinte and north of muddy York. Crops were poor in the first few years, and in 1787 famine struck. But the Loyalist settlements survived, and in 1791 the new province of Upper Canada was created. Its first lieutenant governor was John Graves Simcoe, late of the Queen's Rangers.

LEFT: *Considered a brilliant military strategist, Colonel John Graves Simcoe (1752-1806) served with the British forces during the American Revolution. He commanded the Queen's Rangers from 1777 to 1781. When Upper Canada came into being in 1791, Simcoe was appointed first governor of Upper Canada.* (METROPOLITAN TORONTO LIBRARY)

OPPOSITE PAGE: *Admiral Horatio Nelson, Duke of Bronte (1758-1805). Nelson's dreams of a life with Mary Simpson faded as he left the bustling port of Quebec in 1782. He later became a national hero after he defeated a Spanish fleet off Cape St. Vincent in 1797 and virtually destroyed the French fleet in the Battle of Aboukir Bay one year later. In 1805, he defeated a combined French and Spanish fleet decisively at the Battle of Trafalgar.* (PAINTING BY JOHN RIGAUD)

🕭 NELSON IN LOVE

A dejected Nelson sails from Quebec,
forsaking love for duty.

AS HE STROLLED THROUGH the streets of Quebec, which
had been captured by his hero James Wolfe some 20 years before, Horatio
Nelson began to feel the benefits of the bracing fall air. "Health," he wrote
his father, "that greatest of blessings, is what I never truly enjoyed until I
saw Fair Canada. The change it has wrought, I am convinced, is truly wonderful."

In the winter of 1781 the young Captain had been so worried that poor
health would deny him the fame he sought, that on occasion he came close
to despair. Recuperating at the medicinal springs at Bath on his return from
an expedition against the Spaniards off the Mosquito Coast, he told a friend
that "I have been so ill since I have been here that I was obliged to be
carried to and from bed with the most excruciating tortures... I am phys-
icked three times a day, drink the waters three times and take the baths
every other night, besides not drinking wine which I think the worst tor-

ture of all." He complained that his fingers were "as if half dead" and his legs bothered him. But, his doctor assured him that it would eventually "all go off" and that it would not be long before he could go to sea again.

The son of a Norfolk clergyman, he had first gone to sea at age the age of 12. As a midshipman, he had sailed to the Arctic and the West Indies, acquiring the skills he would be expected to master: the ability to go aloft with the topmen, spread sails, fire and gun drills, weighing anchor, and hoisting the longboats. He slung his hammock on the gun deck and sat at table in the dim light with his messmates, sharing the appalling shipboard fare. A boy Nelson's age, who was to die in a fall from the rigging, told his parents:

"Indeed we live on beef which has been ten or eleven years in corn and on biscuit which makes your throat cold in eating it thanks to the maggots which are very cold when you eat them, like calves-foot jelly... We drink water of the colour of the bark of a pear-tree with plenty of little maggots and weevils in it and wine which is exactly like bullock's blood and sawdust mixed together... Indeed, I do not like this life very much... I hope I shall not learn to swear, and by God's assistance I hope I shall not."

He sailed to India aboard the *Seahorse* and saw action for the first time when she came across a ship flying the flag of Haidar Ali, the Muslim ruler of Mysore. Worn out by fever and seasickness, he fell into a deep depression. "I felt impressed with a feeling that I should never rise in my profession," he wrote years later. "My mind was staggered with a view of the difficulties I had to surmount and the little influence I possessed could discover no means of reaching the object of my ambition." Aboard the *Dolphin*, he experienced a sudden transformation of feeling. "A glow of patriotism was kindled within me," he recalled, "and presented my King and Country as my patron. 'Well then,' I exclaimed, 'I will be a hero and, confiding in Providence, I will brave every danger.'" Thereafter, he was rarely to doubt that he was a man of destiny.

At Bath, Nelson was soon fit enough to enjoy the pleasures of the town, attending soirées at the elegant new Assembly Rooms on Lansdowne Hill and performances at the Orchard Street Theatre. When he visited his doctor's consulting room in Gay Street to settle his medical bill, the doctor refused payment. "Pray, Captain Nelson, allow me to follow what I consider to be my professional duty," he said. "Your illness, sir, has been brought on by serving your King and Country and, believe me, I love both too well to be able to receive any more."

A few weeks later, he travelled to Woolwich dockyard to take command of the *Albemarle*, a captured French merchantman re-rigged as a 28-gun frigate. He praised her lines as "clean and bold." Although he was satisfied with his crew, not a man of which he "would wish to change," they were by no means willing hands. For the most part, they were merchant seamen, East Indiamen, which he had ruthlessly pressed into service. Returning to the London docks sailing in line ahead, Nelson had fired a blank charge across their bows as they approached the Channel. In their eagerness to escape, they let out full sail, but when the master of the leading ship saw the *Albemarle's* gun ports open and the guns run out, he and the ships behind him hove to. The unfortunate seamen, so near to reaching home, were bundled aboard the *Albemarle* and two other ships under Nelson's command. They were soon sailing to Cork to escort a convoy across the Atlantic.

"I want so much to get off from this confounded voyage," Nelson wrote to his father. "My doctor has informed me that if I were sent to a cold, damp climate, it would make me worse than ever." To his surprise, he found that crossing the Atlantic in summer agreed "better with me than I expected." As the *Albemarle* entered the St. Lawrence, he and his crew delighted in a climate that was new to most of them: dry, bracing air, warm, sunny days and crisp nights. They sailed past wooded hills, tidy villages graced with slender church spires, and narrow fields running in long strips down to the river. When the ship anchored below the Citadel on July 1, 1782, his life took on a new aspect. For the first time, Nelson fell in love.

Her name was Mary Simpson and she was 16 years old. The daughter of Colonel Saunders Simpson, the provost marshal of the garrison, she lived with her family in an imposing stone house near the St. Louis Gate. Although no portrait of her exists, she must have been something of a beauty as suggested in a hymn of praise published in the *Quebec Gazette*:

"Surely you will listen to my call,/Since beauty and Quebec's fair nymphs I sing./Henceforth Diana is Miss Simpson see,/As noble and majestic is her air…"

Quebec was a military town and Mary Simpson was actively involved in its lively social life. There were balls and musical evenings, skating parties and sleigh rides to Montmorency Falls. The officers "got up" theatricals, held regattas, played cricket, drank to excess and gave dances in the Mess. A colonel's lady describes the scene:

"The society is very much French, elegant, hospitable, and frivolous, while the tone of morals is vitiated by the large number of soldiers. There are balls nearly every night kept up to a late hour, four or five, and the young ladies run about to each other's houses to discuss their conquests of the previous evening after they have arisen at eleven o'clock. If they are in the house they are sitting in their drawing rooms elegantly dressed while officers lounge in after breakfast and remain for hours, generally in the afternoon escorting the young ladies to the public promenades, or to the drives in the neighbourhood in their tandems."

After a day of parades and the firing of salutes, Nelson met Mary at a ball held at the Chateau St. Louis to celebrate the 22nd anniversary of the coronation of King George III. She evidently found him attractive and his attentions flattering, but she had to admit that he was rather "stern of aspect." He was 24 now, "the merest boy of a captain I ever beheld," an acquaintance recalled. "And his dress was worthy of attention. His lank, unpowdered hair was tied in a stiff Hessian tail of extraordinary length and the old-fashioned flaps on his waistcoat added to the general appearance of quaintness of his figure. There was something irresistibly pleasing in his address and conversation and an enthusiasm when speaking on professional subjects that showed he was no common being."

Smitten, Nelson found a confidant in Alexander Davison, a shrewd Scottish merchant and member of the city's legislative council, eight years his senior. He was "violently attached" to Mary, he told him and was determined to marry her. Davison urged caution as Mary showed little inclination to exchange her life as belle of the ball for that of the wife of a young naval captain whose old-fashioned uniform suggested that he was living on little more than his pay.

As summer gave way to fall, Nelson visualized his frigate ice-bound in the river until spring while he sat with Miss Simpson at her fireside in the big house by the St. Louis Gate. Then orders arrived to escort a convoy of troop ships to New York. "A very pretty job at this late season of the year," he complained, "for our sails are at this moment frozen to the yards." On October 13, 1782, he dropped down river to the anchorage to await a wind. The next morning, as Davison was walking to his office near the quay, he was surprised to see one of *Albemarle's* boats alongside and her captain striding into town. When he asked him what had brought him back, Nelson replied, in the flowery language of the time, "I find it utterly impossible to leave this place without waiting on her whose society has so much added to its charms and laying myself and my fortunes at her feet." Davison tried to dissuade him, telling him that "your utter ruin, situated as you are at present must inevitably follow." "Then let it follow," snapped Nelson, "for I am resolved to do it." "And I also," replied Davison, "positively declare that you shall not."

A forlorn Captain Nelson returned to his ship and sailed away to join Lord Samuel Hood's squadron off New York. Dreams of a life with Mary Simpson faded as he wrote to his father, "I think it very likely that we shall go to the Grand Theatre of Actions, the West Indies."

His father expected him to do his duty.

On October 21, 1805, Lord Horatio Nelson defeated the allied French and Spanish fleets off Cape Trafalgar. He would receive a mortal wound in the battle. (U.S. NAVAL MUSEUM)

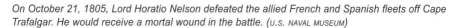

❧ EDWARD AND JULIE

*A martinet and a royal romance leave a
lasting mark in a closely-knit garrison
society.*

SHE WAS QUIET, ELEGANT and well-bred, a victim of the
French Revolution. He was tall and handsome, with a commanding presence and a round Hanoverian face, not unlike his father's, a military man
with a penchant for bands, mechanical toys and hanging his troops.

Julie Thérèse Bernadine de St. Laurent and Prince Edward Augustus,
Duke of Kent, the fourth son of King George III and Queen Charlotte,
and the father of the future Queen Victoria, were the most curious pair to
ever walk the ramparts of a Canadian garrison town.

Providing for the royal succession was far from Edward's thoughts in
August 1791, when he stepped ashore at Quebec with Madame de St.
Laurent and the 7th Royal Fusiliers. Restoring his reputation and winning
the approval of his father occupied his mind, to the exclusion of all else.
That approval had been singularly lacking in his youth. A royal biographer

RIGHT: *Julie, the love of the Prince's life, would remain at home, unable to take part in Edward's public life. When Edward finally married, she retreated to the solace of a convent.*

OPPOSITE PAGE: *Although a strict disciplinarian with his men – he never hesitated to make use of the cat-o'-nine-tails – Edward was known in the social world as a wonderful dancer and musician.*

notes that he had been posted to Canada as "a kind of exile, not unlike the Russian mode of punishing high offenders by sending them to pass their days in Siberia."

Edward had been raised with his brothers the Prince of Wales, the Dukes of York and Clarence and two sisters at Kew Palace. A serious and precocious youngster, he did not fit the pattern set by his boisterous brothers. He resembled the King in many ways, but was never a favourite with either his father or mother. Packed off to Hanover at the age of 17, he followed the example of his older brothers, gambling and falling into debt. He was then sent on to Geneva to be introduced to continental society. "I have been nearly two years in the dullest and most insufferable of all places," he confided to his diary. "The last 17 months of my stay here without a single line from the King and only one letter from the Queen."

In addition to running up more debts, Edward had a love affair and sired an illegitimate child. In January 1790, he gave his mistress and creditors the slip and fled to England. Enraged, his father hurried him on to Gibraltar.

Gibraltar was worse than Geneva. The hot weather distressed Edward, bringing on bilious attacks from which he would later never be free. He performed his military duties adequately, but once again spent beyond his means. "He neither drinks nor games in the least," a member of his staff wrote. "But in certain points of expense such as horses, furniture, etc., he is impatient of control." He also loved music and formed a private band, spending lavishly on instruments and uniforms. Succumbing to boredom, he sent a confidant to France with the decorous mission of "finding a lady to share his bed and preside at his table." At Marseilles, Edward's gentleman friend engaged Madame St. Laurent. Edward was far more fortunate than he deserved or hoped. Julie, supportive and protective, was to be the love of his life.

At Quebec, Edward and Julie settled into an unpretentious stone house near the Château St. Louis. Soon the very centre of the town's social scene with its concerts, balls and levees, Edward and his regiment were acknowledged by the dominating Lady Dorchester, governor Sir Guy Carleton's wife, as "the best dancers, well dressed and best looking figures in a Ball Room I ever saw. They are all musical and like dancing," she wrote, "and bestow as much money, as other Regts. usually spend in wine, in giving Balls & Concerts which makes them very popular in this place…"

Julie, enjoying the ambiguous state of mistress rather than wife, would never appear at any social function in their two-and-a-half year stay in Quebec. She would live all her days with her prince in a strange sort of social twilight.

Charming and affable in the ballroom, Edward favoured spit and polish and rigid discipline in the barracks. "On the parade ground he was a Prussian officer," a soldier recalled. He forbade his officers to travel in the countryside without him, and cursed and struck his troops. Within weeks, he provoked a mutiny. Condemning the ringleaders to death, he dressed them in shrouds and forced them to march behind their coffins to the place of execution before reading a royal pardon. He was recalled to England in 1793.

After brief service in the Caribbean, Edward was appointed Nova Scotia's commander-in-chief, and landed at Halifax in the spring of 1794. He immediately set to work building a spacious town house for Julie on the north flank of Citadel Hill and a cottage on nearby Bedford Basin. Soldiers cleared the woods around the "Prince's Lodge" and adorned it with a pagoda and a lake altered in shape to resemble a heart. Pathways were laid out in sweeping curves to spell the name Julie. She was a "pleasing, sensible woman," the governor said, noting that "she has great influence over him."

Unfortunately, that influence did not extend to military matters. Ever the Prussian, Edward made frequent use of the cat-o'-nine-tails to discipline his troops. On special occasions he would have the entire garrison marched to the Common to witness executions. From the portico of his house he could see the gallows situated near Egg Pond. Stately dinner parties and gay balls were sometimes interrupted by cries in the night.

"Just below, not a hundred yards away, was the North Barrack parade ground," a local historian wrote. "Too often, some poor shivering soldier stood bound to the triangle in a hollow square of comrades to suffer hundreds of lashes. Despite the drowning roll of the drums, his cries were borne upward to the household of the Commander-in-Chief."

From the day he sailed through the Narrows, Edward was determined to transform Halifax into a great fortress. He ordered the top of Citadel Hill to be sheered off to a depth of 15 feet and levelled the ruins of old blockhouses to create a platform for heavy artillery atop a barracks housing 650 men. The Grand Parade was cut down to the level of Barrington Street and new barracks were built along Sackville and Cogswell streets. On George's Island in the harbour, he replaced the old defences with a star-shaped fort mounting 30 guns. The Eastern Battery and Forts Ogilvie and Sackville were repaired and Martello towers built at Point Pleasant and the York Redoubt. The most fortified place in North America, Halifax would become known as "The Warden of the North."

His most innovative creation was a telegraph system using flags and lanterns to connect posts at Chebucto Head and the Dockyard with garrisons across Nova Scotia. Delighted with this new toy, he bombarded officers with orders. On one occasion, he ordered a man flogged at Fort Anne, over a 100 miles away.

Wherever he lived, his quarters were cluttered with music boxes, artificial singing birds, toy organs with dancing horses, and watches and clocks of all kinds. That obsession induced him to build a clock tower on the town side of Citadel Hill. Reminiscent of a giant wedding cake, the tower remains Halifax's best known landmark.

Julie was welcomed by the local gentry and was not subjected to social snubs as she had been at Quebec. She and Edward entertained on a grand scale, although he was deeply in dept. On summer evenings, they rode through town or were serenaded by regimental bands at a little white bandstand, with a gilded cupola and Greek columns, on the grounds of their home.

In the spring of 1800, Edward was allowed to return to England. A week after he and Julie sailed, in a macabre memento of his passing, 11 soldiers he had condemned to death for mutiny were paraded before the garrison. Eight were reprieved in the shadow of the gallows. The others hanged.

The union of Britain and Ireland was imminent and Edward thought that he might be appointed Lord Lieutenant of Ireland. His father thought not, and shipped him off to Gibraltar again, this time as governor. His civil appointment was as disastrous as his military command years before. Like their counterparts at Quebec and Halifax, the soldiers of the garrison mutinied. He was discreetly recalled in 1803.

In 1817, Edward and Julie were forced to part when reasons of state made it imperative for him to marry and provide an heir to the throne. Greatly distressed, he observed: "It is now 27 years that Madame de St. Laurent and I have lived together. We are of the same age and have been in all climates and all difficulties together; I protest that I don't know what is to become of her if a marriage is to be forced on me." Julie lived quietly in a convent in France until her death in 1830.

At Court, all recognition of Julie's existence was ignored and Edward's stay in Canada seldom mentioned. The Queen was not amused.

BELOW AND LEFT: *Many of the fortifications initiated by Prince Edward at Halifax's Citadel, including Martello towers (left), remain to this day.* (CANADIAN PARKS SERVICE)

OPPOSITE PAGE: *"The Battle of Queenston Heights" on October 13, 1812. Engraving by T. Sutherland, based on a sketch by Major James Dennis, 49th Regiment, who took part in the battle.* (PAC/AP C-276)

ᔗ THE WAR OF 1812

British high-handedness and interference in U.S. trade during the Napoleonic Wars leads to war in North America and Canada becomes a battleground.

WILLIAM HAMILTON MERRITT WAS 18 years old when the War of 1812 broke out, living with his parents on a farm near the village of Shipman's Corners about twelve miles from the Niagara River in Upper Canada. War with the United States had long been expected, but when the news reached Shipman's Corners on June 27, nine days after the Americans declared war on Britain, it still took Merritt by surprise. Riding into the village the next morning, he realized his life was about to change. Just weeks before he had been commissioned as a lieutenant in the 1st Troop of the Niagara Light Dragoons, under the command of his father, Major Thomas Merritt.

At Shipman's Corners, his friends and neighbours were milling about discussing the news. "All were in Commotion," Merritt wrote, "as we expected an Immediate attack from the Americans, who, we believed had long been prepared for it." He rode off with his troop to patrol the Niagara River, anxious and worried. The men, he explained, "turned out with a desire and determination of doing their duty, but were acting under the impression of being eventually Conquered."

The war caught Upper Canada unprepared. Acting as temporary civil governor as well as commander-in-chief, General Sir Isaac Brock heard the news while dining with American officers at Fort George just outside of Newark on the Niagara River. Brock insisted they finish their meal, then, with much handshaking and expressions of regret, accompanied his guests to their boats for their trip back across the river to Fort Niagara. Within days they were firing at each other.

Brock faced overwhelming odds, with 300 British regulars and 400 Canadian militia to defend hundreds of miles of frontier. Canada had fewer than 500,000 people from which he could draw recruits, while the United States had a population of more than seven million. Moreover, he was faced with the same problem that had plagued Sir Guy Carleton in 1774: would the people of Upper Canada, many of whom were former Americans, fight the enemy or embrace them? "My situation is most critical, he wrote to the adjutant-general in Montreal, "not from anything the enemy could do but from the disposition of the people – the population, believe me is essentially bad. Legislators, Magistrates, Militia Officers, all, have imbibed the idea that this province must inevitably succumb, and are so sluggish and indifferent in all their respective offices that the artful and active scoundrel is allowed to parade the Country without interruption, and commit all imaginable mischief. I, however, speak loud and look big."

Speaking loud and looking big meant a great deal in this most unusual or wars.

The war that changed the lives of young Hamilton Merritt and Sir Isaac Brock, had been a long time coming. For more than two decades, since the French Revolution in 1789 and the rise of Napoleon, England and France and their allies had been locked in a far-flung conflict which had eventually affected the newly-independent United States. Besides fighting on land and sea, both sides waged economic warfare. Napoleon's Continental Decrees and Britain's Orders-in-Council caught neutral nations in the middle, impeding trade and commerce. In response, the United States prohibited its citizens from trading with either belligerent, but this harmed the American economy more than it did those of the warring nations. There were also problems on the high seas. Britain began to seize cargoes bound for the Continent and maintained her traditional right to search neutral ships for deserters from the Royal Navy. In 1807, when HMS *Leopard* battered the American frigate USS *Chesapeake* into surrender simply to remove four suspected deserters, the two nations teetered on the brink of war. President Thomas Jefferson attempted to diffuse the crisis by passing the Embargo Act, which effectively declared American neutrality.

Added to these problems were troubles with the Indian bands in the northwest, which were desperately trying to turn back a tide of white settlement. Pontiac's rebellion convinced many Americans that Britain was inciting Indian hostility in the hope of recovering the lands ceded to the United States by the Treaty of Versailles. The Americans took a determined stand, defeating the Indians at Fallen Timbers in 1794. Although Jay's Treaty, signed the same year, resolved some of the outstanding differences over the boundary and the western posts, many Americans were convinced that there would be no lasting peace.

Britain, fully committed to the struggle against France, adopted a policy towards the United States that was a masterful combination of arrogance, shortsightedness, and stupidity. America, in British eyes, was a weak, inconsequential nation that could be pushed around with impunity. In the words of the *London Courier*, "two fifty-gun ships would be able to burn, sink and destroy the whole American navy." The British pushed the Americans too far and dismissed their former colonists with an indifference that bordered on contempt. Receiving no redress through diplomacy, President James Madison, supported by a small group of western Congressmen that Thomas Jefferson dubbed the "War Hawks," decided to seek it through military means. On June 18, 1812, with the cry of "Free Trade and Sailors' Rights," the United States declared war on Britain.

It was a war that almost no one wanted. The British, at war with Napoleon on the Continent, tried to prevent it, but when they could not, saw it as more of a troublesome sideshow. Canadians like the Merritts, preoccupied with carving a home out of the wilderness, did not want it, nor did

Henry Clay was a proponent of war as the spokesman of the War Hawks. (PAINTING BY MATTHEW JOUETT, U.S. STATE DEPARTMENT)

New Englanders, who dismissed it as "Mr. Madison's War," and largely sat it out. Nova Scotia issued a proclamation that the province would "abstain from predatory warfare against our neighbours" and carry on trade as usual. The French in Lower Canada saw it as another of the English civil wars in which they had no stake. Apart from the War Hawks, only the followers of the Shawnee chief Tecumseh welcomed the war, hoping to regain the lands they had lost to American settlers in the northwest. This was a wistful dream, doomed to failure.

A war against Britain would mean an invasion of Canada, and the Americans were optimistic. Henry Clay of Kentucky, the most eloquent of the War Hawks, declared in Congress: "It is absurd to suppose that we will not succeed in our enterprise against the enemy's provinces. We have the Canadas as much at our command as Great Britain has the ocean… I am not for stopping in Quebec or anywhere else, but I would take the whole continent from them and ask no favors. I wish never to see peace until we do."

Thomas Jefferson believed that taking Canada would be "a mere matter of marching."

That, too, was a wistful dream. The war lasted for two and half years, growing more and more vicious as it progressed. Towns and villages were despoiled, crops laid waste, and livestock slaughtered. Both sides burned each other's capitals. Although casualties were not high by European standards, thousands of soldiers died on the battlefields, or succumbed to disease. In the course of the war, 7738 Americans and 8774 British and Canadians would lose their lives. By comparison, Napoleon lost 40,000 men at Leipzig in the "Battle of the Nations" in 1814. The Russians lost an esti-

The War Hawks, led by Henry Clay, were vocal advocates of war against England. Congress was eventually persuaded and on June 12, 1812, declared war on Britain. (DETAIL OF THE PAINTING "THE OLD HOUSE OF REPRESENTATIVES," BY SAMUEL F.B. MORSE, CORCORAN GALLERY OF ART)

mated 44,000 men, or one in three participants, in the Battle of Borodino, and 40,000 British and French died at Waterloo.

It was a war marked by incredible bungling. On the American side, superannuated American Revolution generals, long past their prime, engaged in petty rivalries and bitter infighting with green militia officers and political appointees. Secretary of War William Eustis, whose entire department consisted of eight clerks, was an alcoholic incompetent, while the senior commander of the northern frontier, Maj.-Gen. Henry Dearborn, was old, sick, and tired. Maj.-Gen. William Hull, who would lead the march into Upper Canada, was tired too – tired of war, hesitant of command, and suspicious of the untrained and untrustworthy militia who marched with him. Half of the 12,000 men of the U.S. regular army were raw recruits. Worse still, distance, the terrain, and primitive communications created a logistical nightmare – not only was it difficult to move troops to the northern frontier, it was even more difficult to supply them once they got there.

On the Canadian side, the army was led by autocratic British professionals, who had gained their commissions by purchase, not competence. With certain exceptions like Brock, Lt.-Col. John Macdonnell, and Colonel Joseph Morrison, most were castoffs from Europe where the cream of the British Army was fighting Napoleon. Aging veterans, "much given to drink," made up the regular force. The militia, like its American counterpart, was little more than an armed mob, prone to desertion at the first opportunity. Apart from the few flank companies raised by Brock, and Charles-Michel de Salaberry's Voltigeurs Canadiens, most militiamen were relegated to transporting supplies, building roads and fortifications, and guarding prisoners.

The militia's low casualty rate – only 26 were killed in action – gives some indication of its relative worth.

Still, it came to be widely believed that the militia won the War of 1812. The militia myth, as it came to be known, was born with a sermon by the Rev. John Strachan, a few weeks after Brock's death at Queenston Heights, in which he predicted that it "will be told by future historians, that the Province of Upper Canada, without the assistance of men or arms, except for a handful of Regular troops, repelled its invaders, slew or took them all prisoners, and captured from its enemies, the greater part of the arms by which it was defended… Never was greater activity shown in any country, than our Militia have exhibited, never greater valour, cooler resolution, and more approved conduct, they have emulated the choicest veterans, and they have twice saved the country."

In his inimitable style, Egerton Ryerson reinforced the myth in 1880: "The Spartan bands of Canadian Loyalist volunteers, aided by a few hundred English soldiers and civilized Indians repelled the Persian thousands of democratic American invaders and maintained the virgin soil of Canada unpolluted by the foot of the plundering invader."

This was nonsense, but the militia myth would dominate Canadian military thinking for more than a century.

The war ended in stalemate; the status quo ante bellum. The last and bloodiest battle of the war, the Battle of New Orleans, was fought ten days after a peace treaty had been signed at Ghent, Belgium, on Christmas Eve, 1814.

There were two official winners. "The War itself was satisfactory to all parties in that both sides won it," the historian A.R.M. Lower wrote. "The American tradition is one of glorious victories and so it is the Canadian. The British, who did most of the fighting and whose navy was the major instrument in ending the war, have no tradition at all and there are few English people who have ever heard of it."

An unusual war, indeed.

OPPOSITE PAGE: *The charisma and foresight of General Sir Isaac Brock (1769-1812) helped thwart the United States' invasion plans. After ordering the capture of Fort Michilimackinac, he led attacks on Detroit and Amherstburg. He was killed by an American sharpshooter while leading an attack against a battery on Queenston Heights.* (ONTARIO ARCHIVES)

✎ SIR ISAAC BROCK AT QUEENSTON HEIGHTS

A surprise dawn attack by the Americans on October 13, 1812, ends in victory for British and Canadian forces.

WHEN HE READ PRESIDENT James Madison's address to Congress in December 1811, the commander-in-chief of British forces in North America, Lt.-Gen. George Prevost, wrote that it was "full of gunpowder" and showed "such hostility toward England" that he decided to place the provinces "in state of preparation in the event of war." Prevost's command extended over the provinces of Upper and Lower Canada, Nova Scotia, Cape Breton, New Brunswick, Prince Edward Island, Newfoundland, and Bermuda. The lieutenant governors of each of these colonies were responsible to Prevost, who in turn answered to the British government. Besides performing civil functions, Prevost and most of the governors were also military commanders within their jurisdictions, giving British North America a well-established chain of command which Madison and his subordinates lacked.

A veteran of four separate campaigns against the French in the West Indies and an able diplomat, the 44-year-old Prevost had no illusions about the difficulty of his task – he had only 5700 officers and men to defend a vast territory and he could expect no reinforcements from Britain, which was engaged in a mortal struggle with Napoleon. His forces consisted of eight regular regiments of varying strength and a handful of Royal Engineers, with transport and support on Lakes Ontario and Erie provided by the Provincial Marine with five schooners and fewer than a hundred seamen. Of necessity, he would have to fight a defensive war.

Prevost's strategy, like that of Montcalm and Carleton before him, was to hold Quebec at all costs, for Quebec was the key to Canada. To do so, he was prepared to abandon Upper Canada, which he regarded as indefensible and a military liability. Moreover, he was under instructions from London not to engage in offensive operations "except it be for the purpose of preventing or repelling Hostilities or unavoidable Emergencies."

This policy did not sit well with his most capable subordinate, Maj.-Gen. Isaac Brock. A native of Guernsey in the Channel Islands, Brock had been in Canada since 1802 and was not only the military commander of Upper Canada, but also, in the absence of Lieutenant Governor Francis Gore, the civil administrator of the province. An affable, charismatic man, who read the Classics and was equally at home in a barracks room or at a society ball, he commanded respect wherever he served. Hamilton Merritt remembered him as "active, brave, vigilant and determined. He had a peculiar faculty of attaching all parties and people to his person: in short, he infused the most unbounded confidence in all ranks and descriptions of men under his command." Private Shadrach Byfield of the 41st Foot recalled that "our general was very much beloved; he used to come out and talk very familiarly with us." He stood six-feet-four and at 42 was, in his own words, "hard as nails."

Brock favoured a much more aggressive strategy than Prevost. Far from abandoning Upper Canada, he was prepared to take the war to the enemy, to attack and seize American territory that might serve as a staging point for invasion. Brock obeyed orders, though, and directed his energies in the spring of 1812 to strengthening the defences of Upper Canada. He repaired the forts along the border, reinforced the Provincial Marine, which allowed him to move and supply his widely separated forces more effectively, reorganized the militia, and secured the confidence and support of the Indian tribes of the northwest.

Brock was well aware of the bitter enmity between the Americans and the Indians, as well as the reputation of the Shawnee chief Tecumseh, who had managed to unite the tribes into an Indian Confederacy, willing to set aside their differences to fight the hated "Long Knives." Brock first met Tecumseh at Amherstburg in August 1812. "A more sagacious and gallant warrior does not I believe exist," he wrote. "He has the admiration of everyone who conversed with him." Tecumseh's assessment of Brock was more to the point. "This," he told his followers, "is a man!"

The news of America's formal declaration of war arrived in Canada by roundabout means. Prevost learned of it through contacts with John Jacob Astor's fur trading company in New York. It was an inauspicious beginning and British North America was in real peril. To Prevost's adoring daughter, Anne, however, all the portents were good. "I saw nothing before me but my Father's honour and glory," she confided to her diary. "Although I knew how small a force we had to defend the Canadas, such was my confidence in his talents and fortune, that I did not feel the slightest apprehension of any reverse. I thought those abominable Yankees deserved a good drubbing for having dared to think of going to war with England."

Brock was not nearly as optimistic. In Upper Canada, local officials curried favour with American sympathizers, the Iroquois on the Grand River Reserve proclaimed their neutrality, and the Legislative Assembly denied him the power and resources he needed. When the politicians finally went home, Brock promptly declared martial law and set off for war.

On July 5, Brig-Gen. William Hull crossed the Detroit River into Upper Canada with 2500 men and issued a pompous proclamation to its people: "The United States offers you Peace, Liberty, and Security," he intoned. "Your choice is between these and War, Slavery, and Destruction." Unfortunately, the peace, liberty, and security he offered amounted to little more than a swath of destruction that extended as far as sixty miles up the Thames River. His bravado was short-lived, however. With his supply lines threatened and harassed by Tecumseh's warriors, he beat a retreat back to Fort Detroit.

In the meantime, Brock had authorized the commandant at St. Joseph

A view of Fort George from Fort Niagara in 1813, painted by Edward Walsh. (NAC/c-000026)

Island, Captain Charles Roberts, to act as he saw fit on Hull's flank. Like his superior, Roberts was a man of action and moved immediately to take the strategically placed American fort at Michilimackinac, which guarded the passage into Lake Michigan. Without firing a shot, Roberts won a victory that electrified the northwest and rallied the western tribes to Tecumseh's cause.

At Fort Malden, where Brock and Tecumseh had joined forces, the Delaware, Kickapoo, Seneca, Potawatomi, and Wyandot celebrated Robert's victory with a war dance. "It was an extraordinary spectacle to see all these aborigines assembled together at one time," the voyageur Thomas Verchères de Boucherville wrote, "some covered with vermilion, others with blue clay, and still others tattooed from head to foot. A European witnessing their strange spectacle for the first time would have thought he was standing at the entrance to hell, with the gates thrown open to let the damned out for an hour's recreation on earth!"

Convinced by captured documents that Hull was confused in his command, distrusted by his own men, and fearful of an Indian massacre – fear of the Indians was entrenched in American minds – Brock conceived an audacious plan to take Fort Detroit.

With 300 British regulars, 600 of Tecumseh's warriors, and five field pieces, Brock crossed the river and laid siege to the garrison. Parading the Indians around the walls of the fort several times to give the illusion of a much larger force, he then informed Hull by letter that he could not control them if an assault were to take place. "It is not my inclination to join a war of extermination," he wrote, "but you must be aware that the numerous body of Indians who have attached themselves to my troops will be

In response to Tecumseh's driving force, warriors and their families set up camp near British posts. (INDIAN ENCAMPMENT ON LAKE HURON, BY PAUL KANE, ART GALLERY OF ONTARIO)

beyond my control the moment the contest commences."

Afraid of succumbing to the same fate as had befallen Fort William Henry in 1757, when Montcalm lost control of his Indian allies and they brutally murdered at least185 soldiers and civilians following the fort's capitulation, Hull surrendered, giving up 2200 prisoners, 2500 muskets, 33 artillery pieces, and a vast supply of stores. But the greatest benefit of Brock's astounding victory was a change of attitude in Upper Canada. "The militia have been inspired by the recent success with confidence," Brock wrote to his brother. "The disaffected are silenced."

A scapegoat for Washington's bungling, Hull was court-martialled for cowardice and sentenced to death. "I have done what my conscience directed," he said in his own defence. "I have saved Detroit and the Territory from the horrors of an Indian massacre." He was pardoned but spent the rest of his life in disgrace.

With the fall of Detroit, war-fever waned on both sides of the border. On learning that the British government had revoked its restrictive maritime legislation, one of the major causes of the war, Prevost proposed a ceasefire. His American counterpart, Maj.-Gen. Henry Dearborn, agreed and the two commanders signed an armistice on August 9, to remain in effect until their respective governments considered the matter. Madison, however, refused to recognize this agreement, and on September 4 hostilities officially resumed.

The aggressive Brock, who had disliked the idea of a ceasefire, returned to Fort George to prepare for another invasion. It was not long in coming. On the morning of October 13, after a fierce artillery barrage, 5000 American regulars and New York State militia under the command of Maj.-Gen.

Massacre of Americans by Indian warriors. The British use of Indian auxiliaries and the exaggerated tales of their brutality often unnerved the U.S. forces. At Fort Detroit, General Brock used the threat of his warriors to prompt the premature surrender of a much larger American force. (WILLIAM L. CLEMENTS LIBRARY, UNIVERSITY OF MICHIGAN)

Stephen Van Rensselaer, a socially prominent Hudson Valley landowner with "no training beyond the sanguinary prognosis of a dress parade, or a night attack on the café of the old Fort Orange Hotel at Albany," began crossing the Niagara River at Queenston.

"Day was just glimmering," wrote Sir John Beverly Robinson, a young Canadian militiaman and future attorney general of Upper Canada. "The cannon from both sides roared incessantly; shells were bursting in air, and the side of the mountain above Queenston was illuminated by the continual discharge of small arms."

The landing was a disaster. Strong currents scattered or swamped the boats, and those that did make it to the Canadian side of the river came under heavy fire. Witnessing the carnage, many of the militiamen, who, under the constitution, were not required to fight on foreign soil, refused to cross. Others crossed and returned. Still, more than 1200 landed and after a short but severe engagement in Queenston, scaled the heights above the village. Officers were under orders to shoot anyone who tried to retreat.

Brock was awakened with news of the landings at Fort George and was soon in the saddle galloping south along River Road to Queenston. Along the way, he passed the 3rd York Militia marching toward the sound of the guns and groups of American prisoners. "It was one of those uncomfortable, cold, stormy days that mark the end of the season," John Beverly Robinson recalled. "The road was lined with miserable wretches, suffering under wounds of all descriptions and crowding to our houses for protection and comfort." There were also civilian refugees from Queenston flee-

RIGHT: *John Norton, the adopted nephew of Joseph Brant, led the Six Nations Indians at the Battle of Queenston Heights, on October 13, 1812. (*NATIONAL ARCHIVES OF CANADA*)*

FAR RIGHT: *Although leading a vastly superior force, American General William Hull surrendered Fort Detroit to General Brock and his Mohawk allies on August 16, 1812.* (PORTRAIT BY GILBERT STUART, NATIONAL PORTRAIT GALLERY, SMITHSONIAN INSTITUTE)

ing the fighting. Others in the village, like Laura Secord, stayed to help the wounded.

It was now about 7:30 a.m. and daylight. The Americans were in possession of the high ground and the British were reorganizing on the northern outskirts of Queenston. Brock rounded up about 50 soldiers, mostly members of the 49th Light Company and some militia, and led them up the main street to a stone wall below the heights. He then dismounted and, waving his sword, urged them to follow him up the slope, having decided to attack the Americans before they could consolidate their position.

George Jarvis, a 15-year-old volunteer with the 49th, found himself next to Brock. "The British moved upward at double quick time in the very teeth of a sharp fire from the enemy's riflemen," he recalled. Brock, tall, and resplendent in his red tunic and general's cocked hat, made a conspicuous target. Jarvis describes what happened next: "'Ere long he was singled out by one of them (Robert Walcot, an American gunner), who, coming forward, took deliberate aim and fired; several of the men noticed the action and fired – but too late – and our gallant General fell on his left side, within a few feet of where I stood. Running up to him I enquired, 'Are you much hurt Sir?' He placed his hand on his breast and made no reply, and slowly sunk down."

Brock's aide, Lt.-Col. John Macdonnell, renewed the attack, but he too was killed as he approached an American battery. The British retreated in disorder. Young George Jarvis and several others, finding themselves outflanked, threw down their weapons and surrendered.

British command now fell to Maj.-Gen. Roger Sheaffe, Brock's American-born deputy, who arrived on the scene shortly afterwards with the Fort George garrison, a detachment of artillery, and 300 Indian warriors led by Major John Norton, the adopted nephew of Joseph Brant. Realizing that another frontal assault up the wet, muddy slope would be suicidal, Sheaffe deployed his force to the west, where it could approach the heights on more level ground, screened by the trees. The Americans were taken by complete surprise as fire erupted on their left flank, punctuated by Indian war cries. Their ammunition spent, they put up a brief resistance, then crowded back to the river's edge. "They had no place to retreat to," wrote John Beverly Robinson, "and were driven to the brink of the mountain which overhangs the river. They fell in numbers. Many leaped down the side of the mountain to avoid the horrors which pressed on them, and were dashed in pieces by the fall."

On the American side of the river, 3000 New York militiamen refused to move. "The name Indian," an officer wrote, "the sight of the wounded brought off, or the devil, or something else petrified them. Not a regiment, not a company, scarcely a man would go."

Nine hundred and twenty-five Americans surrendered, and there were 250 casualties. The British and Canadians lost only 14 dead and 77 wounded. One of the 14 was Sir Isaac Brock, a grievous loss to the country he had fought so well to defend. Tecumseh, too, lost much with Brock's death, for he was the most outspoken advocate of an Indian homeland. No one would speak with such a voice again.

LEFT: "The Battle for Queenston Heights." Although Brock was killed leading the initial counterattack, he has always been credited with the victory. Painting by J.D. Kelly. (ANNE S.K.BROWN MILITARY COLLECTION)

OPPOSITE PAGE: Handsome, athletic, and an inspired orator, Tecumseh spoke of peace and co-existence. (NAC/C-319)

SHAWNEE SHOOTING STAR

The most revered of Indian chiefs, Tecumseh dreamed of a vast confederacy strong enough to resist American expansion. The dream died at Moraviantown on October 5, 1813.

HIS IMPLACABLE ENEMY William Henry Harrison said of him that "if it were not for the vicinity of the United States, he would perhaps be the founder of an empire that would rival in glory Mexico or Peru. No difficulties deter him. For four years he has been in constant motion. You see him today on the Wabash, and in a short time hear of him on the shores of Lake Erie or Michigan, or on the banks of the Mississippi, and wherever he goes he makes an impression favourable to his purpose. He is now upon the last round to put a finishing stroke to his work. I hope, however, before his return that that part of the work which he considers complete will be demolished, and its foundations rooted up."

If Crazy Horse and Sitting Bull are the most famous American Indians, Tecumseh, the legendary Shawnee chieftain, is the most revered. In the first decade of the 19th century, he dreamed of melding the diverse North American tribes into a vast confederacy, stretching from Canada to the Gulf of Mexico, which would be strong enough to resist the tide of American expansion. A charismatic leader with exceptional military and political abilities, he restored his people's pride in their heritage and culture, and created a powerful Pan-Indian alliance which supplanted tribal rivalries. In the early months of the War of 1812, he and his great admirer, Sir Isaac Brock, saved Canada from almost certain defeat.

Dressed in buckskins, he cut a remarkable figure. No official portrait exists, but reliable witnesses speak of him as "noble-looking," "very prepossessing," and "one of the finest-looking men I ever saw." A little over medium height, handsome and athletic, he exuded energy and purpose. An inspired orator, he swayed all who heard him with his passionate eloquence. Speaking to an audience of Indians and whites in the frontier town of Chillicothe in the Indiana Territory in 1807, a witness recalls that, "when Tecumseh rose to speak… He appeared one of the most dignified men I ever beheld. While this orator of nature was speaking, the vast crowd preserved the most profound silence. From the confident manner he spoke of the intention of the Indians to live in peace with their white brethren, he dispelled as if by magic the apprehensions of the whites."

His speech that day was a plea for co-existence. It was one of his last.

One of seven children, Tecumseh was born in 1768 in the village of Old Piqua, the present-day site of Springfield, Ohio. His father was a Kiscopoke chieftain and his mother a member of the Turtle Band, both clans of the Shawnees. Shawnee names were highly symbolic. Tecumseh is generally translated as Shooting Star or Blazing Comet, and some believe that his name was inspired by the transit of Venus in the year of his birth. The spiritual patron of his clan was a celestial panther, making a strict rendering of his name, A Panther Crouching for His Prey.

As an adult, Tecumseh was noted for his generosity and compassion. He was pragmatic and often ruthless, but he was rarely indifferent to an appeal to humanity. A boyhood friend recalled that he "always expressed the greatest abhorrence when he heard of or saw acts of cruelty." His compassion was remarkable, for his childhood had been ravaged by insecurity, brutality, and war. He knew hunger, fear and grief. The "Long Knives" (as they called Americans), had killed his father and burned his home and he had seen prisoners tortured. In his young manhood, his people, their numbers reduced by smallpox, had been driven north into the Ohio and Indiana territories, losing their lands and much of their traditional way of life. As a warrior, he would mount the most ambitious Indian resistance movement in American history.

Tecumseh was not alone in understanding that if the Indians were to resist American encroachment, they must unite in peace as well as in war. Joseph Brant had attempted to unite the tribes south of the Great Lakes during the American Revolution; and the Shawnee chiefs Blue Jacket and Red Pole had built a shaky confederacy of northwestern tribes. However, Tecumseh stands out for the breadth of his vision and his ability to strengthen his arguments with religion, building upon the foundations laid by his brother, the Prophet.

Slight and sickly, with a disfigured right eye, Lalawethika, the Prophet (who was also known by the name Tenskwatawa), cut a poor figure next to his brother. But it was he, not Tecumseh, who had founded the movement towards a confederacy. He was the medium of the Great Spirit, he said, chosen to show the way to salvation. Tecumseh militarized the movement and became its driving force, but the Prophet remained important, lending it divine sanction.

In 1810, with Britain on the verge of war with the United States, William Henry Harrison, the 38-year-old governor of the newly formed Indiana Territory, grew increasingly alarmed as Indians migrated into Prophet's Town, near Greenville on the Maumee of the Lakes. After a stormy meeting with Tecumseh, whom he had fought at Fallen Timbers, Harrison moved a force along the Wabash and shattered the confederacy at Tippecanoe. Unwittingly, he drove Tecumseh into the arms of the British.

Moving north with 30 followers and gathering recruits along the way, Tecumseh crossed the Detroit River and reached Fort Amherstburg in June 1812. By the time war was declared, he had offered his services to King George III and assembled a force of more than a thousand, including warriors from the Fox, Kickapoo, Delaware, Sauk, and Wyandot tribes.

Regulars and militia under William Henry Harrison attack Prophet's Town on the Tippecanoe River on November 7, 1811. (NAC-C-095294)

Tecumseh's journey coincided with another march north. The Army of the Northwest, 3000 strong, was on its way to Fort Detroit under the command of Brigadier General William Hull. A week after Tecumseh's arrival at Amherstburg, he too crossed the river, with cavalry and heavy artillery, and took the town of Sandwich (present-day Windsor, Ontario). Aside from a minor engagement at the Aux Canards River, where he routed a small force of Indians and regulars, Hull made no move to attack British fortifications. His appetite for war wilted and he beat a hasty retreat back to Detroit when he learned that Tecumseh had ambushed a supply column along the Raisin River.

"Among the Indians whom I met at Amherstburg, and who had arrived from distant parts of the country, I found some extraordinary characters," General Isaac Brock informed the new British Prime Minister, Lord Liverpool, by letter on August 29. "He who attracted most of my attention was a Shawnee chief, Tecumseh, brother to the Prophet, who for the last two years has carried on an active warfare against the United States. A more sagacious or more gallant warrior does not, I believe, exist."

Tecumseh allegedly returned the compliment when they met for the first time. In a story much loved by Canadian historians, he is said to have turned to his people and exclaimed, "This is a man!" when Brock arrived at Amherstburg with reinforcements and proposed to attack Detroit.

Although it was Lalawitheka, The Prophet, who founded the movement towards confederacy, his brother Tecumseh would soon overshadow him.
(PAINTING BY CHARLES BIRD KING)

On the afternoon of August 14, 1812, ignoring the protests of his senior commanders, Brock led a combined force of 1300 Indians and regulars north to Sandwich. Tecumseh crossed the river to Detroit that night, well aware of Hull's indecisiveness and fear of his warriors from documents captured on the Raisin River. At daybreak, Brock came across and the artillery opened fire on the stockade. War whoops rent the air as the garrison huddled behind the palisades. To give the impression that Hull faced an overwhelming force, Tecumseh had his warriors circle the stockade time and again, four or five abreast. Fearing a massacre, Hull struck his colours without firing a shot.

The extent of the victory was soon apparent: Hull surrendered 2188 men, 40 guns, 3000 muskets, and large quantities of stores and ammunition. Brock would receive a knighthood for the capture of Fort Detroit. Tecumseh's reward was even greater. He had seen the Long Knives humbled and Tippecanoe avenged.

That winter, Tecumseh moved south along the Wabash rallying warriors to his cause. In April 1813, when he returned to Amherstburg with 3000 braves, he learned of Brock's death at Queenston Heights and that Major General Henry Procter was now in command.

It was Procter's misfortune to be compared with Brock and found wanting. A 50-year-old Anglo-Irishman, Procter had been a soldier most of his

With little in the way of support from Britain, it was imperative that Isaac Brock succeed in securing the Indian tribes as allies. Tecumseh, shown here defending the whites at Fort Meigs, proved instrumental in organizing the Indian resistance. (ROYAL ONTARIO MUSEUM)

life, but lacked both leadership skills and experience on the battlefield. His difficulties were compounded by his superiors, Sir George Prevost and Major General Sir Roger Sheaffe, who succeeded Brock in the overall command of Upper Canada. Their priority was the defence of the Canadas further east, and Procter was kept short of every item of supply.

The Commander-in-Chief favoured a strictly defensive campaign, but Procter understood that maintaining Tecumseh's support required far more than that. Like Brock, he knew he must take the offensive to present himself as a credible ally.

Major General Procter also knew that inactivity would lead to defeat. "If I tamely permit the enemy to await his reinforcements and mature his plans," he wrote, "he will become too formidable." Accordingly, he laid plans to attack the Americans at Fort Meigs near the Maumee rapids, opposite the site of the Battle of Fallen Timbers.

There were few successes in the campaign that followed. Tecumseh and his warriors were brilliant bush-fighters, but they always found the problems of taking fortified positions largely insurmountable. Feints, ruses and direct attacks on Fort Meigs failed, and Procter was forced to abandon the siege when his militiamen returned home to plant their spring crops.

Contrary to legend, which always portrays the two as enemies, Procter and Tecumseh treated each other with respect. Tecumseh often joined Procter for dinner, mixing easily with the general's wife, daughters and son. However, their relationship deteriorated after the expedition to Fort Meigs.

An irascible man, Procter's temper did not improve during the summer

Johnson's Kentuckians descend on Moraviantown on October 5, 1813. Led by Richard Johnson, the battle lasted only minutes as the American cavalry shattered the loosely-formed British line. Meanwhile, another American column descended on the position held by Tecumseh. The Shawnee chief's death at Moraviantown would lead to the end of Indian resistance south of the Great Lakes. ("REMEMBER THE RIVER RAISIN! BATTLE OF THE THAMES", BY KEN RILEY, NATIONAL GUARD HERITAGE).

of 1813. American attacks along the Niagara frontier and the burning of York threatened his communications and deprived him of supplies. In September, he lost naval supremacy on Lake Erie when Commodore Oliver Hazard Perry defeated a British fleet at Put-in-Bay, allowing Tecumseh's nemesis, William Henry Harrison, to land troops in his rear. When he ordered a retreat to the lower Thames, Tecumseh accused him of cowardice.

Procter's plan had merit, but he implemented it with breathtaking incompetence. He confided in no one, arousing deep suspicions among the Indians. Ordnance and stores were removed. Detroit was abandoned, and Fort Malden and the public buildings at Amherstburg put to the torch. Tecumseh reluctantly agreed to accompany the retreat, although many of his warriors chose to return to their homes.

It began to rain and the roads were churned into a morass. It took three days to reach the mouth of the Thames. Tecumseh rode with the rear guard while Procter rode ahead in his carriage, sending subordinates back down the line with orders. The Prophet, hardly a model of courage himself, told his brother that he felt like ripping the epaulets from his shoulders.

The retreat turned into a rout. Men and equipment were strung out for miles with Harrison and his Kentucky cavalry – hard-riding mountain men armed with long rifles, eager to even the score for Raisin River and Fort Meigs – in hot pursuit. Arms and ammunition were lost and stragglers taken prisoner. Despondency enveloped the troops like a fog. Tecumseh had a premonition that the end was near. "I am weary," he said, "and I feel we shall never leave this ground."

On the morning of October 5, Procter called a halt and turned to fight on the north bank of the Thames, a little below Moraviantown. He had fewer than 500 men now, the ragged remains of the 41st Regiment of Foot, the Royal Newfoundland Regiment and the Tenth Royal Veteran Battalion.

John Richardson, a 16-year-old infantryman and future novelist, recalled that "a few minutes before the American bugles were heard, Tecumseh passed along our line. He was dressed in his usual deerskin dress, which admirably displayed his light yet sinewy figure, and in his handkerchief, rolled as a turban over his brow, was placed a handsome white ostrich feather... He pressed the hand of each officer as he passed, made some remark in Shawnee appropriate to the occasion, and then passed away forever from our view."

When the line broke, he was felled by a single shot. His body was never found.

BELOW: *On October 5, 1813, while fighting at the Battle of the Thames at Moraviantown, Tecumseh receives the pistol shot that took his life. (ROYAL ONTARIO MUSEUM)*

OPPOSITE PAGE: *Henry Procter, unable to live up to his predecessor Brock, would be court-martialled for his incompetence in December 1814. (PAINTING BY J.C.H. FORSTER, DEPARTMENT OF CANADIAN HISTORY)*

THE RISE AND FALL OF GENERAL HENRY PROCTER

Praised and damned, Major General
Henry Procter ended his days in obscurity,
the victim of an old adage.

THE AMERICANS HAD WILLIAM Hull and Henry Dearborn, the British Procter. In a war noted for incompetence at the highest level, these three leaders stand out.

Each was accused of mismanagement and more, after conducting disastrous campaigns. Hull was sentenced to death, then reprieved in recognition of his service during the Revolutionary War. Dearborn was relieved of his command. Procter was suspended from rank and pay for six months and publicly reprimanded, then condemned time and again by succeeding generations of historians.

The beginning of Procter's fall began with Oliver Perry's victory on Lake Erie. No sooner had he cared for the dead and wounded, than he set to work repairing his and Robert Barclay's captured ships to transport Harrison's army across the lake. A regiment of Kentucky cavalry and 4,500 troops

In the heat of battle, Catain Robert Barclay uses his blank-loaded pistol to fire his guns at Perry's ships.
(*DRAWING BY C.W. JEFFREYS, NAC/C-073575*)

were landed below Fort Malden, forcing Procter on to the road to Moraviantown. Never popular in the army, his subordinates savoured his discomfort as Tecumseh accused him of cowardice, likening his conduct to "a fat animal that carries its tail upon its back, but when affrighted, drops it between its legs and runs off."

Procter's courage had not always been questioned. A professional soldier for 30 years, he enjoyed Brock's confidence and had been publicly acclaimed when he led a combined force of Indians and regulars deep into enemy territory to attack Hull's supply line at Brownstown and Maguaga (on August 5 and 9, 1812, respectively). His success reinforced Hull's almost paranoid fear of the Indians and was a factor in his surrender at Detroit. Four months later, Procter annihilated a column led by General James Winchester at Frenchtown, convincing the Americans that they faced another British commander of the calibre of Brock.

As Brock's successor, he moved on to Fort Meigs on the Maumee, savaging Henry Clay's Kentucky militia. Although he was forced to abandon his siege of the garrison when his Indian allies drifted away, he had the satisfaction of knowing that he had forestalled another American invasion of Upper Canada. But his troubles were only beginning.

A scarcity of supplies, ammunition and men soon sapped him of all hopes of maintaining an aggressive stance. He wrote one futile letter after another to his superiors pleading for reinforcements as he watched American strength grow. Adding to his troubles, Tecumseh demanded that he resume the offensive. Against his better judgement, he moved against Fort Stephenson,

On September 10, 1813, Barclay's poorly gunned six ships lost to Perry's well-armed sloops. After the battle, the fleets paused for the sea burial of their dead in Put-in-Bay. (PAINTING BY PETER RINDLISBACHER)

forcing Harrison to retreat. But the cost was high and he lost many of his irreplaceable regulars.

Misfortune continued to dog him. When Captain Barclay sailed to meet Perry at Put-in-Bay on September 10, 1813, he did so with Procter's impressed soldiers and cannons from the forts. The loss of the entire fleet left him in an untenable position. A disheartened Procter abandoned all hopes of holding the frontier and resolved to "retire to the Thames without delay."

American and British accounts of Procter's retreat argue that he was more concerned for his personal safety and that of his family than for his army, and that he fled on the pretext of looking for a suitable battleground. The fact is, his army, hungry and fever-ridden, was bogged down on muddy roads. Moreover, Lieutenant Colonel Augustus Warburton, in charge of the rearguard, dallied and spent most of his time arguing with his subordinates.

At Moraviantown, Procter deployed his troops in good order in a natural defensive position with the Thames to the right and a swamp to the left. Unfortunately, he ignored the fact that his men were totally exhausted. After a single, scattered volley, Harrison's cavalry smashed through the line then wheeled into the swamp to engage Tecumseh and his warriors. The battle was over almost as soon as it began. Tecumseh and three quarters of Procter's men were killed or captured against a loss of seven American dead and 20 wounded.

Procter was accused of positioning himself well behind the British line and having fled for Burlington at the first shot. In fact, he remained with his men to the bitter end, almost to the point of capture. He attempted to rally his men until it became all too evident that they were defeated, and only then did he leave the field.

The disaster at Moraviantown threw Major General Francis de Rottenburg, Commander-in-Chief of Upper Canada, and most of his senior officers into a panic. De Rottenburg ordered a retreat and was prepared to cede the entire frontier west of Kingston. Procter, ridiculed for his "rush to the rear," refused to obey his orders, rallied what remained of his army, and stood fast at Ancaster.

Moraviantown, or the Battle of the Thames, was one of the more spectacular victories of the war for the Americans. In a matter of weeks, Commodore Perry had swept the British from Lake Erie and Harrison had crushed Procter's army. Tecumseh's death sapped the enthusiasm of the Indians for the British cause and most returned to their homes. The Americans were now in control of western Upper Canada, depriving the British of a springboard for further incursions into Ohio and Michigan.

But the fortunes of war are fickle. Three months later, General Sir Gordon Drummond recaptured the entire Niagara Peninsula and put Fort Niagara, Lewiston, Schlosser, Black Rock, and Buffalo to the torch.

Court-martialled at Montreal in December 1814, Procter expressed his disappointment, then faded away into obscurity, yet another victim of an old adage: Nobody loves a loser.

BELOW: *After the battle of Put-in-Bay, crews of both the British and American fleets gather on the shore of Lake Erie for the burial of their officers. (BY L.B. CHEVALIER, ERIE COUNTY HISTORICAL SOCIETY)*

OPPOSITE PAGE: *Laura Secord travelled 32 kilometres to warn Colonel James FitzGibbon of Charles Boerstler's planned assault on Beaver Dams. (PAINTING BY A. BOBBETT, NAC/c-024103)*

✑ THE NIAGARA FRONTIER

The worst fears of James and Laura Secord are realized as armies clash at Queenston and across the countryside.

NOWHERE IN UPPER CANADA, in the spring of 1812, were rumours of war with the United States more repugnant than in the village of Queenston. The busiest trading centre on the Niagara frontier, Queenston, nestled on a shelf of land between the river and the Heights, would be in the front lines. War would ruin businesses and many of the so-called enemy, 200 yards across the river, were friends and relatives.

With the coming of war, the three hundred inhabitants of Queenston had unexpected reason to believe that the fighting would pass them by as all was quiet along the frontier. On Main Street, James Secord continued to deal in flour and potash, and it was business as usual at the Ingersoll Tavern, run by his wife's father. A few miles away, at Stoney Creek, 19-year-old Billy Green helped his father sow the spring crops. Like all Canadians, they rejoiced at the victories at Michilimackinac, Raisin River and Detroit and hoped that the war would soon be over.

But that was not to be. Within months, their worst fears were realized as armies clashed on Queenston Heights and ranged across the countryside.

On the evening of May 26, 1813, less than three weeks after the burning of York, James and Laura Secord and their neighbours watched anxiously as British regulars hurried through Queenston on their way to Burlington Bay. For days they had heard the sound of gunfire as American artillery, firing across the river, levelling the village of Niagara. At Fort George, General John Vincent had ordered a retreat and fired the magazines as 5000 Americans came ashore under the command of General Dearborn, Commander-in-Chief of the Army of the Centre. Within six days, the entire Niagara Peninsula was in his hands and American troops were drinking in the Ingersoll Tavern.

Dearborn immediately set to work organizing an occupation force, a task made easier by the fact that many in the Niagara Peninsula were recent American immigrants. By proclamation, he promised protection to those "who recognized the Government of the United States." Those who failed to cooperate were threatened "with disastrous consequences." More than five hundred signed paroles, some to avoid being drafted into the Canadian militia. A quasi-military force of mounted infantry was organized by a New York sheriff who hastened to Fort George to offer his services in "clearing the frontier of persons inimical to the United States."

With the assistance of turncoats and vigilantes, Dearborn tightened his grip on the Peninsula by authorizing a search for concealed arms and rounding up able-bodied men, civilians and militia alike, as prisoners of war. In the dead of night, his men scoured farms and villages making arrests, looting and abusing the population. Many of those taken into custody were old men or convalescent soldiers.

At Burlington, General Vincent could do little except watch helplessly from afar. Desperately short of supplies and clothing, his men were forced to strip the dead. Visiting the camps, Sir George Prevost was horrified to find the troops in rags, many of them without shoes. Ragged they may have been, but they were eager to do battle.

When Vincent was reinforced with two flank companies of the 104th (New Brunswick) Regiment, he ordered probing attacks to harass the

Americans. Lieutenant Colonel Cecil Bisshop took up position on the heights above Twenty Mile Creek with orders to hold the lake road and form a line of communication with the New Brunswickers and a light company of the 8th Foot. Lieutenant James FitzGibbon requested permission to form a company of rangers to act independently of the main force. One of the most popular officers in the army, the son of poor cottagers and a veteran of the Dutch campaigns, FitzGibbon was swamped with volunteers. Accompanied by a handful of William Merritt's Provincial Dragoons, he moved out to Ten Mile Creek astride the roads to Queenston and Niagara Falls, hitting the enemy where and when he could.

Dearborn's actions in the Niagara Peninsula did little to warm the population to their self-proclaimed liberators. Heartened by Vincent's offensive, they began to provide him with valuable information about American positions and troop movements.

At Stoney Creek, a few miles below Burlington Heights, Billy Green scouted out an American encampment. Overhearing the password "Will-Hen-Har" – a derivative of the name of their general, William Henry Harrison – he circled the camp and identified a regiment of cavalry and two brigades of infantry. Almost 2000-strong, he noted that they were poorly organized and that the sprawling camp was barely guarded. Hurrying into Burlington with the news, he forgot the password as he approached American pickets. Years later, he recalled: "I pulled my coat over my head and trotted across the road on my hands and feet like a bear." He reached the British lines a little after dark.

Leading 700 handpicked men from the 8th and 49th regiments, Vincent struck the Americans at midnight. With fixed bayonets, they charged into the camp routing the entire force. Four companies of infantry and a troop of Dragoons took up the chase, hounding the frightened Americans as they discarded weapons and baggage and ran for their lives. "By dawn," Billy Green said, "we could see Americans running in all directions." Now known as Billy the Scout, he joined in the pursuit. American casualties included 17 dead and 38 wounded. Two generals and 100 other ranks were taken prisoner.

Dearborn was so unnerved by the defeat at Stoney Creek that he withdrew his detachments from Chippewa and Queenston, razed Fort Erie,

With bayonets fixed, men of the 8th and 49th Regiments struck at midnight on 6 June 1813 in the Battle of Stoney Creek. (C.W. JEFFERYS, NAC/C-070260)

and pulled his army back into a single fortified camp at Niagara.

All along the frontier, the Americans were coming under attack. At Fort George, Captain Dominique Ducharme and a company of Mohawk volunteers swept down on a tavern taking several prisoners. At Queenston, they surprised a boat crew, killing two and capturing six. FitzGibbon, establishing his headquarters at Chippewa, raided Fort Erie with a company of regulars and 80 Indians. Much annoyed, Dearborn ordered Colonel Charles Boerstler of the 14th U.S. Infantry to rout him out.

Moving at night with a force of 600 men and a battery of light artillery, he passed through Queenston, putting the town under guard. Not unnaturally, his arrival excited the curiosity of the residents, among them James and Laura Secord. Wounded in the fighting at Queenston Heights, James was an officer in the Lincoln Militia and the son of United Empire Loyalists. Like his wife, he had little love for the Americans and immediately guessed their objective. Unable to do so himself, his wife set out to warn FitzGibbon.

Thirty-eight years old and the mother of five, Laura left the house before dawn with a pail under her arm, passing sentinels under the pretence of milking a cow in the fields beyond. Out of sight, she threw the pail away and crossed the fields into the woods. A waning moon lit her way to the village of St. David's where she paused to rest at the home of a relative. She then continued her journey, keeping off the roads until she came to a branch of Twelve Mile Creek. At daybreak, she crossed the creek on a tree trunk and scrambled up the far bank into an Indian camp.

The startled warriors leapt from their bedrolls and took up arms, terrify-

With the Mohawk warriors as his allies, Lieutenant James FitzGibbon accepted the American surrender at Beaver Dams. (METROPOLITAN TORONTO LIBRARY BOARD)

ing her. "I cannot express the awful feeling it gave me," she recalled. "I was determined to persevere. I went up to one of the chiefs, made him understand that I had great news for Lieutenant FitzGibbon and that he must let me pass his camp, or that he and his party would all be taken. The chief at first objected to let me pass, but finally consented, after some hesitation, to go with me to FitzGibbon's station. When I had an interview with him, I told him what I had heard – that the Americans intended an attack upon the troops under his command and would, from their superior numbers, capture them all."

Laura Secord's report was almost immediately confirmed by a scout who had sighted American troops near St. David's. FitzGibbon hurried his men into the woods near Beaver Dams and waited. Marching in the early morning sunshine, Boerstler tightened up his column as he approached a gully in a dense forest known as the Beech-woods. Suddenly, he came under heavy fire. Mounted infantry were blasted out of their saddles as Boerstler desperately tried to deploy his men, ordering the artillery and cavalry to the rear. Alarmed and confused as Indians broke cover to take scalps, the troops in the lead fell back into the centre. Boerstler succeeded in restoring some order and regrouped his men in a clearing to the right of the road. The artillery opened fire with grapeshot as he formed the infantry into a single file and advanced. He did not get far.

FitzGibbon's rangers and Ducharme's Mohawks opened fire on his right flank forcing him back into a hollow. Hit in the thigh and bleeding profusely, Boerstler did his best to rally his men. An hour later, surrounded, and with his ammunition running low, he surrendered, unaware that a relief column was on its way from Queenston. Five hundred Americans were captured along with two field pieces and the colours of the 14th U.S. Infantry.

The loss of Boerstler's column and the defeat at Stoney Creek put an end to the American campaign in 1813. Dearborn retreated into Fort George while the British and Canadians steadily eroded American morale with nightly raids – "circumscribing the enemy" in Sir George Prevost's words. He was relieved of his command by an angry Congress and his successor strictly enjoined from taking offensive action until American naval forces could be reinforced on Lake Erie. Billy Green went back to his farm and Laura Secord returned home "exhausted and fatigued."

As with most heroes and heroines, historians and fanciful biographers have chipped away at their reputations. One who never contested Laura Secord's courage was the "brave and noble" FitzGibbon with whom she remained friends until his death. "Mrs. Secord was a person of slight and delicate frame and made her effort in weather excessively warm, and I dreaded at the time that she must suffer in health in consequence of fatigue and anxiety, she having been exposed to danger from the enemy, through whose lines she had to pass," he wrote in a formal deposition. Honoured in her lifetime, she lived into her 93rd year. Appropriately, she is buried in Drummond Hill cemetery at Lundy's Lane.

Billy Green died in obscurity.

LEFT: *Laura Secord walked through forest, streams and marshes to warn James FitzGibbon of the approaching American assault. After stumbling into a Mohawk camp, she eventually solicited their support and warriors were dispatched with her to Beaver Dams. (ILLUSTRATION BY HENRY SANDHAM, NATIONAL ARCHIVES OF CANADA)*

OPPOSITE PAGE: *The capital of Upper Canada, York served as military headquarters for General Brock. (PAINTING BY SEMPRONIUS STRETTON, NAC)*

ᔖ THE BURNING OF YORK

*A pleasant little town of about 1000
souls, York was barely defended in April
1813. The destruction of Government
House and the Parliament Buildings
would set an evil precedent.*

TO TAKE CANADA, THOMAS Jefferson said, was "a mere matter
of marching." But the former president had not counted on the likes of
Tecumseh and Isaac Brock. Detroit and Queenston Heights, along with
humiliating defeats at the River Raisin and Michilimackinac had shocked
Americans into a thorough reappraisal of their hopes for an easy victory.

Incompetence had been the norm in 1812. Winfield Scott, a future Commander-in-Chief of the U.S. Army, recalled that "the old officers had, very
generally, sunk into either sloth, ignorance or habits of intemperate drinking." Opponents of the government were excluded from command and
able men passed over in favour "of swaggerers, dependants, and decayed
gentlemen, utterly unfit for any military purpose whatever."

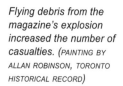

Flying debris from the magazine's explosion increased the number of casualties. (PAINTING BY ALLAN ROBINSON, TORONTO HISTORICAL RECORD)

With a few exceptions, the British army was just as poorly led. Most of the senior officers were Wellington's castoffs who had reached their rank by purchasing promotion. As military surgeon, William 'Tiger' Dunlop observed, "any man whom the Duke deemed unfit for the Peninsula was considered quite good enough for the Canadian market."

Still, they had held their own in 1812 against formidable odds.

The American army in 1812 could muster 17,000 regulars in three divisions: General Henry Dearborn commanded the Army of the Centre, stationed along the shores of the Great Lakes from Buffalo to Sackets Harbor; Wade Hampton commanded the Army of the North at Lake Champlain; while command of the Army of the West, based at Fort Meigs on the Maumee River, was shared by Generals William Henry Harrison and James Winchester. Although they could call on large reserves of citizen soldiers for periods of service of 60 days to a year, most refused to serve outside their home states and for longer than their designated term.

Numbers were somewhat misleading. The British, although vastly outnumbered, had an additional force of more than 2000 Indians under arms along the Niagara Frontier and could call upon the service of a long-term militia. The Incorporated Militia of Upper Canada was made up of young men obliged to serve where circumstances warranted and were recruited for the duration. In Lower Canada, the Select Embodied Militia was composed of men aged 18 to 25, who were required to serve for a maximum of two years. British forces were also supplemented by regular units recruited in Canada such as the Glengarry Fencibles and the Provincial Corps of

The most common form of punishment in the British army was flogging, with the cat-o'-nine-tails.
(RECONSTITUTION BY EUGENE LELIEPVRE, PARKS CANADA)

Light Infantry, better known as the Voltigeurs. When properly trained, they could fight as well as the British, as the Voltigeurs did at Châteauguay.

Both sides were engaged in a frantic naval race, realizing that the outcome of the war depended on control of the lakes and the vital St. Lawrence lifeline. If the Americans could cut that lifeline, Canada would surely wither and fall. To do so was the basis of American strategy throughout the war. "Separated from the rest of the empire by an ocean, and having to this but one outlet," U.S. Secretary of War John Armstrong said, "the St. Lawrence River forms your true object or point of attack."

On February 8, 1813, Armstrong presented a plan of campaign to cabinet noting that the United States did not have the resources at hand to attack along the St. Lawrence. "We must choose between a course of entire inaction because we are incompetent to the main attack," he said, "or we must select a secondary, but still important, object." He urged "the reduction of Upper Canada" and called for an attack on York, the provincial capital, followed by landings in the Niagara area. The cabinet approved his plan two days later and General Henry Dearborn was ordered to begin massing troops at Sackets Harbor to embark with Isaac Chauncey's naval squadron as soon as Lake Ontario was free of ice.

Dearborn, a veteran of the Revolutionary War, hardly inspired confidence. Weighing in at 300 pounds, he had become so gross that he had to be trundled about in a two-wheeled device dubbed a "dearborn" that was later adopted by Midwestern farmers. His opposite number at York, Major General Roger Hale Sheaffe, though slimmer, was so hated by his men for his harsh discipline that they had mutinied. He did not wish to fight the Americans and had asked to be posted elsewhere as he had relatives in the New England States. But fight them he did as they came ashore, 1700 strong, at the mouth of the Humber River.

York, a pleasant town of 1000 souls, was not well defended. Isaac Brock had planned to build a fort but had to content himself with a temporary magazine, a blockhouse and a ditch enclosing Government House and the barracks. It was garrisoned by the flank companies of the York militia, a few gunners of the Royal Artillery and weak companies of the Glengarry Light Infantry, the Royal Newfoundland Regiment, the 8th Foot, dockyard workers and a few Indians. A mixed bag of about 700 men.

In the early morning hours of April 27, Chauncey's fleet rounded Gibraltar Point. "It presented an elegant and imposing appearance," a witness recalled. Moving westward on a gentle breeze, each ship towed a barge to land troops. The residents of York took alarm. Children were hurried indoors, and valuables and family heirlooms hastily buried in backyards. At the Parliament Buildings, clerks squirreled away documents and public funds while militiamen scurried off to join their units.

As the fleet fired a barrage of grapeshot and canister, the Americans came ashore near the present-day site of the Canadian National Exhibition. Forming up under the command of General Zebulon Pike, a former western explorer for whom Pike's Peak would later be named, they set off along the lakeshore, sweeping aside Indians and Grenadiers. Beating a hasty retreat, at least two drowned when they plunged through the rotting ice of what would come to be known as Grenadier Pond.

Falling back on the Western Battery, the remaining Grenadiers opened fire on the advancing Americans, supported by a pair of ancient guns with broken trunnions. Resistance came to an abrupt end when a gunner accidentally dropped a match into the magazine. "Every man in the battery," a soldier recalled, "was blown into the air, and the 'dissection' of the great part of their bodies was inconceivable shocking!"

Lacking leadership, the defenders began to melt away. "There was no person to animate them nor to tell them where they were to make a stand," Peter Finan, the young son of an officer of the Royal Newfoundlanders, said. "The officers knew nothing of what was to be done, each was asking of another, enquiring after the General and running after his aides and messengers in order to ascertain what they should do. In the meantime, the General walked backwards and forwards on the road... more than half a mile from the troops."

Sheaffe had already decided to yield the town to the Americans and retreat to Kingston with whatever troops he could rally. As he marched away, he watched the smoke rising from the partially completed warships in the dockyard that had been set on fire at his order. Leaving the British flag flying, he had also given orders to fire the Grand Magazine on the shores of the lake.

Pike had halted his column less than 100 yards away and was interrogating a prisoner when the magazine exploded. Finan recalls that the earth shook and "a great confused mass of smoke, timber and earth rose in a most majestic manner and assumed the shape of a vast balloon." More than 400 men in both armies were killed or maimed, General Pike dying beneath a piece of fallen masonry.

The people of York were not sorry to see Sheaffe leave. His competence was questioned, and he had never won the popularity that Brock enjoyed. The Americans, however, would soon be even less popular.

Enraged by Pike's death and Sheaffe's escape, they gave themselves over to looting and pillaging, joined by republican sympathizers and prisoners released from the jails. Households were wrecked and public buildings set afire. Legend has it that angry American sailors set fire to the Parliament Buildings after mistaking the Speaker's wig for a scalp. The town was "pillaged dismal" a resident recalled. Claims to the provincial government included such items as furniture, linen, silverware, tools, tobacco, and liquor. When Joseph Hendrick saw his schooner go up in flames, an embarrassed Dearborn paid him for his loss with public funds seized from the treasury. But few others were as fortunate.

By the time they embarked on May 2, Dearborn and his men had set an evil precedent. In the months to come, Newark and Forts Niagara, Buffalo and Black Rock would be put to the torch. And in August 1814, Washington would burn.

❧ BATTLE OF CHÂTEAUGUAY

A few weeks after the Battle of Châteauguay the second arm of the invasion met with the same fate... defeated by a much smaller force.

TO THE DEFENDERS OF Upper and Lower Canada, October 1813 was a time of near despair. American warships ranged the Great Lakes at will, forcing Sir James Yeo's Lake Ontario squadron into Burlington Bay and seizing six of seven schooners carrying troops to York. The loss of Lake Erie following Commodore Oliver Perry's victory at Put-in-Bay imperilled Michilimackinac and the entire west. Newark and York lay in ruins and the Thames River valley was a wasteland. Now, a powerful American army had gathered at Sackets Harbor and another waited at Plattsburg on Lake Champlain, ready for the stroke that Prevost feared most: a coordinated attack on Montreal.

Fortunately, incompetent and vainglorious generals continued to frustrate the best-laid American plans. Far from occupying Upper Canada after

RIGHT: *Huddled in blankets near a fire, the Voltigeurs wait at Châteauguay.* (ILLUSTRATION BY EUGENE LELIEVRE, CANADIAN PARKS)

OPPOSITE PAGE: *Charles - Michel d'Irumberry de Salaberry (1778-1829), a Canadian soldier, was commissioned in the British army in 1794 and served in the Napoleonic Wars. He returned to Lower Canada in 1810 and commanded the Voltigeurs.* (PAINTING BY DONALD GUTHRIE MCNAB, MUSÉE DU CHÂTEAU RAMEZAY, MONTREAL)

his victory at Moraviantown, General William Harrison had sent his militia-men home to Kentucky with their grisly trophies and come east to bask in glory. Instead of attacking Kingston, which would have effectively cut the supply lines to the west, General Henry Dearborn wasted the summer raid-ing York and skirmishing on the Niagara Frontier. Dearborn had at long last been relieved of his command, but his successor, the old and lethargic General James Wilkinson had a reputation as an unreliable scoundrel. True to form, he ignored orders to take Kingston, decided on the advance to Montreal, then fell ill after arriving at Sackets Harbor with a mountain of baggage. Worse still, the commander at Plattsburg, General Wade Hamp-ton, the most despised man in the U.S. Army, was Wilkinson's sworn per-sonal and political enemy.

The 70-mile march north from Plattsburg soon proved too great a strain for Hampton's ill-prepared force of more than 5000 regulars. Summer had given way to a cold, rainy fall, and the men had only their summer uni-forms. They also had to contend with a lack of water. One officer com-plained of being "compelled to abandon clothing and other things essen-tially necessary to preserve the body in health." By the time they arrived at Four Corners, just below the Canadian border, the supply system had bro-ken down.

On September 25, Hampton made camp, having learned of Wilkinson's illness, and busied himself improving the cart track to Plattsburg. Five days later, his outlying pickets were ambushed. "The attack had a bad effect on the morale of the army," wrote Colonel Robert Purdy of the 4th U.S. Infan-try Regiment. "The soldiers contracting an absurd dread of a foe who, though despicable in numbers, was unseen and unsleeping. The men shrank from sentry duty, and not a night passed without dropping shots from the woods. To this natural fear was added discomfort. No new clothing was issued, and the cotton uniforms for summer wear, now threadbare and ragged, were poor protection against the white frost and the rains of fall. Food had to be hauled from Plattsburg, keeping 400 wagons, drawn by 1000 oxen constantly on the road, so the supply was subject to the weather and often short."

The "unseen and unsleeping enemy" that so concerned Colonel Purdy were Canadian Voltigeurs and Caughnawaga Indians under the command of Charles-Michel d'Irumberry de Salaberry.

The burly, ebullient son of a Lower Canadian seigneur who had fought the Americans in 1775, de Salaberry had been a soldier all his adult life, serving in England, Ireland and the Caribbean. Three of his brothers also held commissions in the British army, and all three died on active service. As an officer with the 60th Regiment of Foot, he had developed tactics to make rifle companies mobile, hard-hitting, and flexible – tactics that flew in the face of the traditional British thin red line. Back in Canada, he had the opportunity to put his theories to the test when he was called upon to form the Voltigeurs, a force recruited primarily from the local habitants and armed with rifles instead of muskets.

The name Voltigeurs was derived from the French "to leap" or "to vault." As much at home in the woods as their ancestors who had fought *la petite guerre*, de Salaberry trained them to move fast, strike hard, then disengage. Clad in grey, with black bearskin caps, they had become a formidable body of light troops that fought best alongside Indian warriors in the hit-and-run of forest warfare. "The true rifleman will never fire without being sure of his man," de Salaberry told them. "And he will recollect that a few direct shots that tell will occasion greater confusion than a thousand fired at random." Once again, he would soon have an opportunity to test his theories.

After weeks of waiting, Hampton was informed that Wilkinson had finally struggled out of his sick bed and planned to set off with 8000 men in an armada of boats down the St. Lawrence. He was ordered to advance to the mouth of the Châteauguay River "or other point, which shall favour our junction and hold the enemy in check."

As soon as Hampton crossed the border, his lead units began to be sniped at and he found the roads blocked with felled trees. Meanwhile, pickets along the river had sent word to de Salaberry that Hampton was on the move and he quickly marched south with two companies of Voltigeurs, one of Canadian Fencibles, a mixed French and English unit, and 22 Indians. On October 24, he was reinforced by Lieutenant Colonel "Red George" Macdonnell with the First Light Battalion of Lower Canada after a remarkable three-day trek from Kingston. To Dr. William "Tiger" Dunlop, who passed them on the road, they "presented a serviceable effective appearance – pretty well-drilled, and their arms in perfectly good order, nor had they a mobbish appearance."

De Salaberry chose to face the Americans on the ravines along the Châteauguay River, near the present-day village of Allan's Corners. While Hampton's main force slowly struggled forward, he set his 300 or so men to work to prepare a defensive position; a series of breastworks and an abatis of sharpened tree branches, similar to the one Montcalm had used with such deadly effect at Carillon in 1758.

On the morning of October 25, as de Salaberry and his men watched and waited, the first Americans emerged from the trees into the stump-dotted clearing in front of the abatis. In the eerie silence, de Salaberry sent a runner to warn Macdonnell of a possible flank attack, then moved along the line, talking calmly to his men and exuding confidence. As he did so, a mounted American officer galloped forward to within shouting distance of the waiting Canadians and, in poor French, demanded they surrender. De Salaberry seized a rifle from one of the Voltigeurs and fired, dropping him from his horse in mid-sentence. He then ordered his men to open fire.

As volley after volley crashed into the American lines, de Salaberry leaped onto a stump to direct the battle, instructing his officers to use French, "so that they might not be understood by the enemy." The Caughnawaga warriors on his right flank raised their whooping cries, and he ordered his buglers to sound the "advance." Macdonnell, who was in the first reserve line, then "caused the bugles to be sounded in all directions, so as to induce the enemy to believe that we were in far greater numbers."

The ruse worked. As de Salaberry's men looked on in disbelief, the Americans wheeled about and retreated, leaving 70 dead, hundreds of wounded, and 16 prisoners behind. By nightfall Hampton's army was back in its encampment and every cart trail along the Châteauguay was strewn with discarded equipment, drums, provisions, and muskets. "I write you just a word to let you know that the enemy commenced his retreat," de Salaberry wrote to his wife, Anne. "I believe that we have saved Montreal for this year... I hope they are going to let us rest and that I shall have the happiness to see you shortly. I am very tired. I kiss you a thousand times, also the little one."

Although the Americans were indeed retreating, de Salaberry thought they might simply be regrouping. For the next eight days, he and his men stayed behind their barricades, waiting in the cold autumn rains. The weather became a worse enemy than the Americans. "We suffered so much from foul weather that some of our men fell sick every day," wrote Lt. Charles Pinguet. "I now know that a man can endure without dying more pain and hell than a dog. There are many things that I can tell you easier than I could write them, but you will be convinced by this affair that Canadians know how to fight."

Charles-Michel de Salaberry had taught them well.

BELOW: *On October 26, 1813, de Salaberry and his Voltigeurs successfully repulsed General Wade Hampton at Châteauguay. (PAINTING BY H. DE HOLMFIELD, MUSÉE DU CHÂTEAU RAMEZAY, MONTREAL)*

OPPOSITE PAGE: *Lieutenant Colonel Joseph Wanton Morrison (1783-1826) commanded the "corps of observation" that brought Wilkinson's army to ground at Crysler's Farm. (MCCORD MUSEUM)*

◆ THE BATTLE OF CRYSLER'S FARM

As the Crysler family huddled in a root cellar, Joseph Morrison fought a set-piece battle. His victory on November 11, 1813 resounded throughout the Canadas.

AS THE SUMMER OF 1813 gave way to fall, Sir George Prevost, the Commander-in-Chief in British North America, was a very worried man. Along the Niagara frontier, at Sackets Harbor and the Four Corners, American armies were gathering and intelligence reports indicated that Prevost would soon face a major offensive. "The forces now assembled by the enemy at different points for the purpose of invading these provinces is greater than at any other period during the war," he wrote to the colonial secretary, Lord Bathurst. A few weeks later, Commodore Oliver Perry defeated the British fleet on Lake Erie and Major General Henry Procter's army was swept away at Moraviantown.

At Prescott, Colonel Thomas Pearson, an irascible veteran who had fought in Egypt, the Netherlands and Spain, was more confused than worried. An

The people of Prescott, Ontario, continued to trade with their American neighbours in Ogdensburg, New York, throughout the war. (DRAWING BY WILLIAM HENRY BARTLETT, NAC C-002339)

attack must come, he knew, but where? For more than six months he had not allowed his garrison to undress at night in case of attack, and expressed the wish that if the Americans came down the river, "he would get some account of them." In early November, he dispatched Lieutenant Duncan Clark to Elliot's Point to observe any movement along the river with instructions that "on the appearance of an enemy," he was to "instantly take horse, and repair to Prescott, with all possible diligence, alarming the country as you pass down."

On the evening of November 5, the young lieutenant spotted an American armada of "some 300 of every description of craft, including several gunboats," and, mounting a borrowed plough horse, rode off at a furious pace to carry out his orders.

The war had scarcely touched the valley of the St. Lawrence, strategically because the American command had mounted its major offensives in the west and locally because the people, Americans and Canadians alike, heartily disapproved of it. To many Americans it was simply "Mr. Madison's War."

There was, of course, some war fever. The sons of old Loyalists rallied to the colours and there were skirmishes at Ogdensburg and Gananoque, and Prevost had bungled an attack on the naval base at Sackets Harbor in the early days of the war. But for the most part, it was business as usual. Colonel Pearson, far from discouraging this amiable state of affairs, actually encouraged fraternization and had been a frequent guest at dinner parties on the American side of the river. That abruptly came to an end with the appointment of John Armstrong as Secretary of War.

American transports and gunboats on the St. Lawrence River.
(LITHOGRAPH AFTER COKE SMYTH, ROYAL ONTARIO MUSEUM)

Armstrong, a 54-year-old veteran of the Revolutionary War and the author of *Hints to Young Generals by an Old Soldier*, fancied himself a strategist. Citing the Swiss theorist Antoine-Henri Jomini and his emphasis on concentration of force, he began to assemble troops and naval supplies at Sackets Harbor throughout the summer of 1813 in order to launch a "grand invasion" of Canada. The first objective would be Kingston, followed by a swift descent down the St. Lawrence to join forces with an army advancing up from Lake Champlain and the Richelieu River. The combined forces would then move on to Montreal.

The plan was in many ways similar to Jeffrey Amherst's during the Seven Years War. If Armstrong knowingly adopted Amherst's strategy, he missed the essential point: Amherst had left Lake Ontario secure behind him, whereas he, failing to take Kingston, would have to cope with a constant threat to his rear. Moreover, his generals were grossly incompetent.

Major General James Wilkinson, Commander-in-Chief of the Northeastern Army, was, in the words of his biographer, "as utterly destitute of all real honor, as venal, as dishonest, as faithless as any man that ever lived." Wade Hampton, his counterpart on the Lake Champlain front, was not much of an improvement. A slave-owning southerner, reputedly the richest man in the United States, he was universally despised and would not communicate with Wilkinson except through third parties. Nonetheless, they would pose the most serious threat to Canada in the entire course of the war.

As word spread along the river that the Americans, 8000 strong, were on the move, Captain William Mulcaster of the Royal Navy sailed out of Kingston with a squadron of gunboats and 60 bateaux carrying a hastily assem-

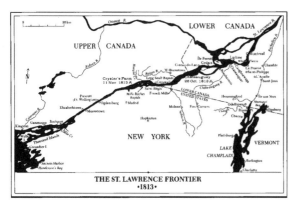

This map shows the divisions of territory along the St. Lawrence River, between Upper and Lower Canada and the United States in 1814.

bled "corps of observation" commanded by Lieutenant Colonel Joseph Morrison.

Respected and liked by both superiors and subordinates, the 30-year-old Morrison had actually seen very little action during his 14 years in the army. The same could not be said of his second-in-command, John Harvey, who was a veteran of countless campaigns and the victor at Stoney Creek, nor of James FitzGibbon, the hero of Beaver Dams, and Pearson, who joined them at Prescott.

Although outnumbered ten to one, they commanded the best units in Canada: the 49th, Brock's old regiment, and the 89th Foot. Known as the "Green Tigers" from the facings on their tunics, the 49th had been the mainstay of the defence of Upper Canada in the past year, fighting at Queenston Heights and Fort George, Stoney Creek and Black Rock. Reinforced with contingents of Canadian Fencibles, Voltigeurs and 30 Mohawk warriors, they set off with orders to "pursue and harass the enemy."

The Americans swept down river in a stately procession five miles long, flags waving and boatmen singing. Thomas Rideout, a Commissariat officer, watched in amazement from the Canadian shore as they passed Johnstown. "It was a grand sight to see them going down the Gallette Rapids," he said. "They fired several shots at us, taking our wagon for artillery, I suppose. Every boat had a gun mounted, and carried 60 men. About 200 immense boats went down full of men, besides schooners with provisions... The Americans seemed confident of taking Montreal. I never witnessed such a beautiful sight as that army going down the rapids."

Running past Prescott and the guns of Fort Wellington under cover of darkness, the flotilla anchored at the Red Mill four miles below Ogdensburg

Topographical map of area surrounding Crysler's Farm. The entire site was flooded in the 1950s by the St. Lawrence Seaway.

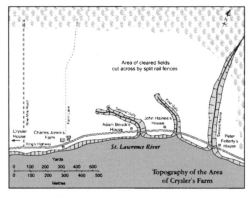

on the morning of November 6. Here, Wilkinson received the news that Hampton had been checked at Châteauguay. Undaunted, he pressed on to the Long Sault.

Wilkinson had not had an easy journey. Down with dysentery, he had taken to his cabin to give council to his fears. He had little faith in his own army and knew that if he was held up for too long, Morrison and Mulcaster would catch him from the rear. Moreover, every militiaman and farmer from Leeds to Glengarry was firing at him at every narrow stretch of the river. Impressed with "the active universal hostility of the male inhabitants of the country," he retaliated by landing infantry to clear the shoreline.

Although Wilkinson's flotilla was passing through some of the most splendid scenery in North America, it was unlikely that the troops were paying much attention to the view. Cold, sick and wet, they were packed into the boats amid casks, crates and barrels of provisions. One soldier recalled that the "flotilla was very much in disorder." An officer explained that "the Commander-in-Chief had arranged on paper, with the most perfect precision, the manner in which the flotilla should move, and perhaps saw no difference between a sheet of paper and a sheet of water."

As he approached the Long Sault, eight miles of white water which he could not traverse in a day, Wilkinson put a force ashore a little below Captain John Crysler's well-tended and prosperous farm to keep the British and Canadians at bay. While Colonel Winfield Scott moved off down the road to Cornwall, Brigadier General John Boyd and 4000 men, "all the well men excepting a sufficient number to navigate the boats," were landed to form a rearguard. After enduring a night of sleet and rain, they formed up on the morning of November 11, unaware that Morrison was waiting for them, determined to stand and fight on ground of his own choosing.

Morrison had chosen his position well, on ground that would allow him to fight a set-piece battle and bring the full firepower of the British line to bear. He had taken a calculated risk to hazard a battle, banking on drill and discipline to offset heavy numerical odds.

A muddy field of winter wheat stretched out a half-mile in front of the Crysler house, cut with gullies and bisected by a stream that trickled out of a swamp into a deep ravine running down to the St. Lawrence. Morrison's right, resting on the river, was covered by Mulcaster's gunboats, and his left, anchored on the swamp, was screened by Indians and Voltigeurs. The centre, astride the King's Road to Montreal and protected by a heavy fence of cedar logs, was held by the 89th with one gun, and the 49th a little to the right and front with another gun manned by Canadian militia. Skirmishers were placed well forward to draw the Americans towards the main force.

A little after two o'clock, as the Crysler family huddled in their root cellar, the Americans advanced. As they emerged from the woods along the left flank, Morrison executed the first of a series of parade ground manoeuvres, wheeling the 89th from its position in line to face them. Raked by a volley, the Americans broke and ran.

Thwarted on the left, General Boyd now marched three brigades across the field in an attempt to turn the British right. Their morale already sapped by the storm the night before, the American troops struggled forward in ankle-deep mud, tumbling into gullies and clawing their way out of the ravines. Morrison's 49th, ordered into echelon in another familiar drill, met them with rolling volleys supported by the field guns.

The action now became a general, confused melee, half obscured by dirty-grey smoke. American dragoons were repulsed in another drill-book manoeuvre as familiar commands rang out over the crash of muskets and canister: "Halt! Front! Pivot! Left wheel into line! Fire by platoons from the centre to the flank!" The effect was shattering as frightened horses reared, their saddles empty. At the same time, a light company of the 89th charged the American artillery, capturing a six-pounder and killing its crew. The American line gave way and the survivors fell back toward the river.

"The fate of the day was decided by this action," Colonel Harvey wrote in his official report. "Some efforts were still kept up, but the fire of our platoons and guns, and above all, the steady countenance of the troops, finally drove the enemy out of the field; and about half-past four o'clock he gave up the contest. The enemy's loss in this severe action in killed, wounded, and prisoners, may be safely estimated at 600 or 700 men. Nearly 180 of the dead were counted on the field; upwards of 100 prisoners are in our hands, and the number of slightly wounded who were carried off is very great."

The stricken American army retreated to the boats and made off as quickly as possible. With his demoralized and disheartened troops, Wilkinson, who had not left his bed during the battle, abandoned the advance on Montreal and moved into winter quarters at French Mills on the Salmon River. Soon after, he was relieved of his command.

There was jubilation throughout the Canadas at the news from Crysler's Farm. Church bells rang and newspapers ran special editions. The *Kingston Gazette* expressed the "highest satisfaction in announcing this glorious event" and praised Morrison's troops who had "displayed the true spirit of British soldiers, which can never fail of asserting its superiority over the enemy whenever he has the temerity to risk a trial."

And in Montreal, a much-relieved Sir George Prevost issued a general order "to be publicly read at the head of every regiment of regular troops and battalions of militia."

"Morrison," he said, "had earned himself a place on 'a field of glory.'"

Detail of a mural by Adam Sherriff Scott of the Battle at Crysler's Farm. (ST. LAWRENCE PARKS COMM.)

🎺 BATTLE OF LUNDY'S LANE

One of the bloodiest battles of the War of 1812 was fought in stifling summer heat within sight of Niagara Falls.

BY THE SUMMER OF 1814, the deadwood had been cleared away from the American high command. Generals Hull, Rensselaer, Dearborn and Hampton had been replaced by younger, more competent officers. Jacob Brown, the new commander of the Army of the North, was several cuts above his posturing and indecisive predecessors. Known as "Smuggler Brown" for his peacetime adventures in the potash trade, he was quick, aggressive and determined, qualities that had served him well at French Mills and Sackets Harbor. When ordered to renew the offensive on the Niagara frontier, he did so willingly and with confidence.

For months, American troops had been training at Buffalo under the watchful eye of Brown's subordinate, Major General Winfield Scott. For ten hours a day, like Baron Friedrich von Steuben at Valley Forge, he subjected officers and men to squad, company and battalion drill until they

RIGHT: *Believing he would be facing ill-trained militia, British General Phineas Riall cried out, "Those are regulars, by God!" at the sight of his enemy.* (PAINTING BY H. CHARLES MCBARREN, U.S. ARMY CENTRE OF MILITARY HIST.)

OPPOSITE PAGE: *The Battle of Lundy's Lane, on July 25, 1814, was the bloodiest of the war on Canadian soil, with almost 1500 casualties.* (PAINTING BY ALONZO CHAPPE, NAC/C-12093)

could manoeuvre in the woods and on open ground with the utmost precision. An esprit de corps began to develop as their military proficiency, morale and health improved. An army surgeon remarked that "even the demon diarrhea appeared to have been exorcised by the mystical power of rigid discipline and strict police!"

Singing "Row brothers row, the rapids are near and the daylight's past," they crossed the Niagara River, 5000 strong, on the night of July 3, sharing Brown's confidence that they would soon be in York.

There had been changes in the high command in Canada as well. De Rottenburg, Vincent, and the despised Sheaffe had been replaced by Sir Gordon Drummond, Prevost's second-in-command, and the fiery General Phineas Riall, a short, stout Irishman, impetuous to the point of rashness. Guarding the Niagara frontier with a long, thin line of regulars, fencibles, and militia, Riall was at his headquarters at Fort George when he was informed that the Americans had landed.

Scott was the first ashore, followed by Eleazer Ripley and his second brigade. Marching inland, they encountered little resistance. Fort Erie, its works open and indefensible on the landward side, surrendered after firing a few shots for honour's sake. As Scott moved on to Chippewa, American militia took up positions at Lewiston to threaten Queenston and Fort Niagara and tie the garrisons down.

Like Brock before him, Riall immediately took horse to meet the enemy, rousing the troops along the way. The Royal Scots, the senior regiment in the British army and known to all as "Pontius Pilate's Bodyguard," was dispatched down the Queenston road along with the 8th Foot, the Lincoln militia and Captain William Merritt's Niagara Light Dragoons. Merritt had just sat down to dinner with his parents at Twelve Mile Creek to celebrate his twenty-first birthday when he was ordered out. At Fort George, he found "everything in activity, and all the troops which could be spared filing off on the road to Chippewa."

At Chippewa, Colonel Thomas Pearson and his men burned the bridges and did what they could to slow the American advance. North of the river, they joined forces with Riall at sunset and dug in. Meanwhile, Scott called a halt at Street's Creek and arranged for a belated Fourth of July dinner and dress parade.

The next day, Riall crossed the Chippewa and moved south in column, assured by Drummond that he would be facing ill-trained militia. He was quickly disillusioned as the Americans wheeled into line with steadiness and precision. As the British advanced, Scott held back his centre and extended his wings, exposing Riall's men to fire from the front and flanks. Enfiladed from three sides, the column disintegrated, a startled Riall crying out, "Those are regulars, by God!"

In less than two hours of desperate fighting, Riall lost 505 men, including 148 killed. Merritt, who arrived after the battle was over, found every house filled with wounded. "I stopped at Street's and spent a very unpleasant night," he wrote in his journal. "Many of the officers were lying wounded, groaning with pain. Such was the result of the battle of Chippewa."

Conceding Chippewa to the Americans, Drummond was still not prepared to give up the Niagara peninsula. He ordered additional troops to Fort George and set sail from York with the Glengarrians to take personal command. The militia turned out, leaving their hay uncut. Morrison, the victor at Crysler's Farm, arrived with the 89th as the 103rd and 104th marched from Burlington. Prevost dispatched the 6th and 82nd from Kingston.

Two days after his victory, Scott moved northward, turning Riall's position and forcing him back on Fort George. Queenston was occupied and an anxious Brown climbed the Heights to scan the waters of Lake Ontario. At the end of a long and vulnerable supply line, he needed the support of

Isaac Chauncey's fleet, unaware that Chauncey, snug in Sackets Harbor, had no intention of allowing his ships to transport supplies. "I have looked for your fleet with the greatest anxiety since the 10th," Brown wrote. "For God's sake let me see you... At all events have the politeness to let me know what aid I am to expect."

As the days passed and Chauncey failed to appear, Brown was forced to live off the land. Foraging parties, led by the turncoats Joseph Willcocks and Benajah Mallory, raided farms and villages and engaged in a deadly guerrilla war with the militia. "The militia were daily skirmishing and driving in the American parties who were plundering every house they could get at," Merritt wrote. "Bewildered families were obliged to leave their homes and place themselves under the protection of the army."

Major Daniel McFarland of the 23rd U.S. Infantry wrote to his wife that the Americans and Canadian renegades had "plundered and burnt everything. The whole population is against us; not a foraging party but is fired on, and not infrequently returns with missing numbers." On July 19 every house between Queenston and Niagara Falls was burned, including forty at St. Davids. To his credit, Brown promptly dismissed the officer responsible.

Riall was kept well informed of what was happening in the American army by deserters and scouts commanded by Captain James FitzGibbon of Beaver Dams fame. Under orders from Drummond not to act precipitately, he shadowed Brown as he abandoned Queenston and moved south towards Chippewa.

On the morning of 25 July, startled to learn that British troops were moving along the river towards his supply depot at Fort Schlosser, Brown instructed Scott to turn around and move his brigade towards the Falls. As he neared Lundy's Lane, a road running at right angles from the Portage Road up and over a gentle slope, he caught sight of Riall's army spread out in a wide crescent around a red frame Presbyterian church with a small graveyard to the right and an orchard below. Deploying for battle, he sent a message to Brown to bring the rest of the army forward as quickly as possible.

Aware that the Americans were about to attack, Riall, still under orders not to provoke a battle, began to withdraw. Arriving on the scene moments later, Drummond immediately countermanded his previous order and hur-

Lieutenant General Sir Gordon Drummond succeeded General Roger Sheaffe as administrator and commander of the forces in Upper Canada, 1813-1815. (PORTRAIT BY GEORGE BERTHON, GOVERNMENT OF ONTARIO ART COLLECTION)

ried the artillery into position on the slope near the church along with the Royal Scots and a company of the 41st. The Glengarrians were dispatched to the right, the 8th and Incorporated Militia to the left. By the time Scott sent out skirmishers, Drummond and Riall were ready and waiting.

Drummond had scarcely completed his dispositions when his centre and left were hit by Scott's full force a little after six o'clock. The gunners broke up charge after charge, scattering the 11th and 22nd Infantry and mauling the 9th. In desperate hand to hand fighting, the 89th, Royal Scots, 8th and 41st, "with the most perfect steadiness and intrepid gallantry," resisted all American attacks. On the left, Major Thomas Jessup's 25th Infantry was more successful. Circling the woods east of the Portage Road, they out-flanked the militia and a handful of Royal Scots.

General Riall was captured as he was being led to the rear with a wound which would cost him an arm. Merritt was also taken prisoner by "six fellows who were skulking from the fire which then raged with great fury." The British re-formed facing the road, secured their flank and repulsed American attempts to get behind the 89th.

At sunset, Brown came up with two brigades while Drummond was reinforced by the 103rd and 104th regiments, the headquarters company of the 8th and a detachment of militia. After "a short intermission," the fighting resumed with renewed fury.

Possession of the guns near the church was the key to success or failure

Jacob Brown, knicknamed "Smuggler Brown" for his peacetime adventures in the potash trade. He was quick, aggressive and determined, qualities that had served him well at French Mills and Sackets Harbor. When ordered to renew the offensive on the Niagara frontier, he did so willingly and with confidence. (ENGRAVING AFTER PAINTING BY ALONZO CHAPPEL, NAC/C-100390)

and the Americans made a determined effort to seize them. Masking their advance in the gathering dusk by an attack on the south face of the slope, Miller's 21st broke through with a bayonet charge. "Our artillerymen were bayoneted by the enemy in the act of loading, and the muzzles of the American guns were advanced within a few yards of ours," Drummond recalled. "Our troops, having for a moment been pushed back, some of our guns remained in the enemy's hands; they were, however, not only quickly recovered, but the two pieces, a six-pounder and a five-and-a-half-inch howitzer, which the enemy had brought up, were captured by us."

In the darkness, confused artillerymen limbered enemy guns. "At one point," Drummond noted, "one of the enemy's six-pounders was put by mistake on a limber of ours, and one of our six-pounders limbered on his, by which means the pieces were exchanged."

Casualties mounted as the British charged the hill with the order "level low and fire at their flashes." Scott had three horses shot beneath him before he went down with a wound to his shoulder and was carried from the field. Brown was hit twice and Morrison gravely wounded. Drummond was shot in the neck, his wound described as "very severe... and very troublesome." Refusing treatment, he led his men in yet another charge. His troops exhausted and ammunition running low, Brown ordered a retreat. Midnight descended upon Lundy's Lane with sporadic rifle fire, then silence.

Although Drummond remained in possession of Lundy's Lane, there was no cheering from the British ranks. Lundy's Lane was not only a hard fought battle, it was a costly one, the most bloody of the War of 1812 on Canadian soil. Drummond reported 600 killed and wounded; Brown 171 dead, 573 wounded and 109 missing. Although claiming victory, he retired to Fort Erie, burning Street's Creek and Chippewa and dumping his baggage in the river along the way.

Sergeant James Commins of the 8th Foot described the battle of Lundy's Lane as "the most obstinate I was ever in, the Yankees was loath to quit their position, and being well fortified with whisky made them stand longer than ever they did. Some of them was so drunk as to stagger into our lines, but they suffered from their temerity." The scene the next morning was one that he never forgot.

"The morning light ushered to our view, a shocking spectacle," he recalled. "Men and horses lying promiscuously together, Americans and English, laid upon one another, occasioned by our advance and retreat... It was found impossible to bury the whole so we collected a number of old trees together and burned them – which, although it may appear inhuman, was absolutely necessary and consequently justifiable."

Then, shouldering his musket, he marched off down the Erie Road.

LEFT: *"The morning light ushered...a shocking spectacle. Men and horses lying promiscuously together, Americans and English, laid upon one another," wrote Sergeant Commins of the Battle of Chippewa. (PAINTING BY F.C.C. DARLEY, BROWN UNIVERSITY LIBRARY)*

OPPOSITE PAGE: *Doctor William "Tiger" Dunlop, surgeon in the War of 1812. (PORTRAIT BY DANIEL MACLISE, FROM A GALLERY OF ILLUSTRIOUS LITERARY CHARACTERS)*

TIGER DUNLOP, SURGEON

A regimental surgeon recalls his battle experiences at Crysler's Farm, Lundy's Lane and Fort Erie.

A GIGANTIC, FLAMING red-haired Scot, the regimental surgeon of the 89th Foot fell in love with Canada at first sight. In time, he would earn fame as a tiger-hunter in India, a parliamentarian, and as Warden of the Woods and Forests with John Galt's Canada Company. A critic of Responsible Government, which he epitomized as "a trap set by knaves to catch fools," he sat as a member of the first Legislature in the United Canadas. A witty raconteur and diarist, known as the Tiger, he would earn the affection and respect of soldiers and settlers alike in the adopted homeland he served so well.

In the spring of 1813, 21-year-old William Dunlop, fresh out of medical school, was biding his time in Parkhurst Barracks on the Isle of Wight waiting for transport to Canada to join his regiment. Many of his fellow soldiers, reluctant reinforcements for the 89th Foot, or Blayley's Blood-

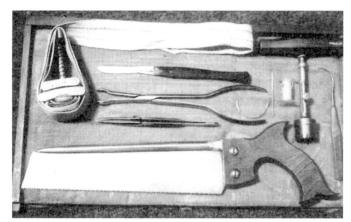

A typical British surgeon's amputating kit included a saw, knife, scalpel, forceps and a tourniquet. (CANADIAN MUSEUM OF HEALTH AND MEDICINE, TORONTO HOSPITAL)

hounds, had successfully postponed the trip for months – no great achievement, for if the August sailing could be conveniently missed, a man was safe until the following April. One soldier had managed to miss every ship for three years.

Dunlop was not as resourceful, nor did he wish to be. After three weary months of sea aboard "a small, ill-found, undermanned and over-crowded tub," he arrived in Quebec in November, a few days before the Battle of Crysler's Farm.

Making his way up river, he took command of a makeshift hospital near the battlefield and began to tend the wounded. "My patients gradually began to diminish," he wrote. "Some died, and these I buried – some recovered by the remedies employed, or in spite of them, and these I forwarded to Montreal." A month later, he moved on to Fort Wellington at Prescott.

Garrison duty was more to his liking. As he whiled away the winter, "walking, lounging and flirting with all that a neighbourhood with a mill, a shop, a tavern and two farmhouses could afford," he recorded that "we rarely went to bed without a respectable quorum of the officers getting a little to the lee side of sobriety."

Rum was plentiful and so was beef, regularly supplied by Americans crossing the river with herds of cattle and no qualms about trading with the enemy. "From the St. Lawrence to the ocean, an open disregard prevails for the laws prohibiting intercourse with the enemy," Major General George Izard, the commanding officer of the Lake Champlain frontier, complained to the War Department. "The high roads are found insufficient for the

Lieutenant Colonel George Macdonnell, known as "Red George" for his colouring, commanded the Canadian troops of the Glengarry Light Infantry, the 1st Light Battalion of Lower Canada. He served Britain well in the War of 1812, distinguishing himself in several battles, including Châteauguay. He also led the attack across the ice against Ogdensburg in February 1813. Vastly experienced, he was one of the best officers in the British army. (NATIONAL ARCHIVES OF CANADA)

supplies of cattle which are pouring into Canada. Like buffalo, they press through the forests making paths for themselves."

Dunlop witnessed a deal being made by his company commander, "Red George" Macdonnell, late of Châteauguay, with a trader who must have been "a kind of Yankee gentleman for he wore his hat in the parlour and spat on the carpet." The deal was quickly closed and payment made in gold. The trader, who was also a major in the Vermont militia, informed him as he was leaving that "they do say that it is wrong to supply an inimy and I think so too; but I don't call that man my inimy who buys what I have to sell, and gives a genteel price for it." Canadian traders shared the sentiment and drank "to a long and moderate war."

The Tiger reserved his criticism for the high command. "In those days Sir George Prevost filled the vice-regal chair of His Majesty's dominions in British North America, and a more incompetent Viceroy could hardly have been selected for such trying times," he wrote. "Timid at all times, despairing of his resources, he was afraid to venture anything; and when he did venture, like an unskilled hunter, he spurred his horse spiritedly at the fence, and while the animal rose he suddenly checked him, baulked him in the leap he could have easily cleared, and landed himself in the ditch. Thus he acted at both Sackets Harbor and Plattsburg, New York, where he was in possession of the forts when he ordered the retreat to be sounded, and ran away out of one side of town while the enemy were equally busy in evacuating at the other."

With the return of warmer weather, Dunlop was ordered to the Niagara frontier, 280 miles away, where a force of 4000 Americans under General

LEFT: *Under the command of William Drummond, the British finally succeed in storming the main bastion of Fort Erie.* (PAINTING BY E.C. WATMOUGH, CHICAGO HISTORICAL SOCIETY)

OPPOSITE PAGE: *The magazine at Fort Erie explodes, inflicting heavy casualties on both sides.* (DRAWING BY A. BOBBETT, NAC/C-0023)

Jacob Brown had crossed the border and quickly captured Fort Erie. Setting off by boat from Kingston and claiming "considerable dexterity both in stealing boats and in managing them when stolen," he was forced to continue his journey by land when a storm drove him ashore. As good horses were reserved for senior officers, he promoted himself to major-general, commandeered a magnificent roan and galloped into Newark on July 25, 1814, just as the wounded were pouring into town from the Battle of Lundy's Lane.

Setting up a hospital in a ramshackle building known as Butler's Barracks, he immediately set to work with the few instruments he had carried with him, persuading a few reluctant local women to take on orderly duties. He worked all through the night as wagon after wagon came down the river road and, by morning, had treated 220 wounded men. He did his best, but by his own admission many lost a limb because he had neither the supplies, nor the time to avoid amputation. "Many had to be laid on the straw on the floor," he recalled, "and these had the best of it, for their comrades were put into berths, one above the other, as in a transport or packet, where it was impossible to get around them to dress their wounds, and their removal gave them excruciating pain."

In the summer heat, swarms of flies infected the wounds of new arrivals and maggots infested the dressings of those already attended to. Whiskey

was the only anesthetic. Working around the clock for two days and nights, Dunlop fell asleep on his feet on the morning of the third day, "my arm embracing the post of one of the berths. It was found impossible to awaken me; so a truss of clean straw was laid on the floor, on which I was deposited, a hospital rug thrown over me, and I slept soundly for five hours without even turning."

The casualties were soon cleared and Dunlop joined his regiment as they laid siege to Fort Erie. The fort had been strengthened since the Americans captured it in July and now included a series of palisades, a log abatis and outlying batteries at Snake Hill. A siege line had been established around the fort, running from the fast-flowing Niagara River to the Lake Erie shore.

Dunlop was exasperated by the lack of initiative of the regulation-bound British regulars who sweltered in the open in their serge, brick-red tunics and refused to follow the example of the casually-dressed Canadian militia who quickly made themselves at home in lean-to shelters. The militia displayed an ingenuity and independence that appealed to him, as they fired from cover behind trees and stumps, oblivious to the Duke of Cumberland's dictum that the infantry must not conceal itself "since battles are not won by jack-in-the boxes." The Canadians also demonstrated the revolutionary idea that rifles were not, as the War Office still held, mere instruments for mounting bayonets.

At two o'clock on the morning of August 14, after a preliminary bombardment, the British and Canadians assaulted Fort Erie form all sides. One column attacked the battery at Snake Hill, another rushed the fort, and a third, the fortified battery on the riverbank outside the walls. The main assault was under the command of Lt.-Col. William Drummond of the 104th Foot. Dunlop went into action with the 89th, festooned with brandy-filled canteens to comfort the wounded.

Three attempts to take the fort failed, before a fourth managed to break into a bastion. A stalemate ensued, in which the British, try as they might, could not break into the main fort, while the Americans could not dislodge them. Then, shortly before dawn, a magazine exploded.

The Americans, protected by the walls of their barracks were largely spared, but British losses were appalling. More than 900 men were killed or wounded. Drummond was later found dead and six battalions were so badly shattered that they were no longer fit for field duty. Dunlop described the effects of the blast:

"After the blow up, our little corps was broken up, and the companies composing it joined their respective battalions. My own regiment was wretchedly reduced; little more than three months before it had gone into the Battle of the Falls, 500 strong, with a full complement of officers. Now we retired about 60 rank and file, commanded by a Captain, two of the senior Lieutenants carrying the colours, and myself marching in the rear – voilà… His Majesty's 89th Regiment of Foot."

On November 5, fearing another attack, the Americans blew up what was left of the fort and withdrew across the river to Buffalo.

The British and Canadians retreated to miserable winter quarters at Queenston. Shelter was inadequate, supplies scarce, and quartermasters were forced to requisition food and fuel from the resentful residents. Malaria, typhus, dysentery, and pneumonia swept through the camps and more than a third of the men were too ill to fight. During the war, more would die of disease, vaguely described as "ague" or "swamp fever," than all the battles combined. Ill-fed and ill-housed, the healthiest were frequently mutinous and large numbers deserted to the United States. Dunlop escaped to York and set up a hospital in the ruins of the Parliament Buildings, which had been burned by the Americans the summer before. Here, in January 1815, he learned that the war was over.

"One of the many blunders of this blundering war," he wrote, "was the Medical and Commissariat Staffs were never where they were needed." The dregs of the army, he called them, of little use in Canada and unfit for service with Wellington in Spain.

Looking back on his service, he recalled: "There is hardly on the face of the earth a less enviable situation than Army Surgeon after a battle, worn out and fatigued in body and mind, surrounded by suffering, pain and misery, much of which he knows it is not in his power to heal or even to assuage. While the battle lasts these all pass unnoticed, but they come before the medical man afterwards in all their sorrow and horror."

The sorrow and horror would haunt the Tiger for the rest of his life.

RIGHT AND BELOW: *The ghastly effects of cannon fire and the impact of heavy lead musket balls were captured in Napoleonic-era drawings by British Army physician Charles Bell. Men suffering wounds of this nature as often died of shock as from the gangrene and infection that invariably set in.* (ROYAL ARMY MEDICAL CORPS MUSEUM, LONDON, ENGLAND)

❧ MR. MADISON'S WAR

Not every American approved of the war. In New England, disagreement with the war was so pervasive that a secessionist movement began.

IN 1812, BRITAIN POSSESSED the most powerful navy the world had ever known. Hundreds of warships were in commission, a result of the long, drawn-out war with France. For more than twenty years the Royal Navy frustrated Napoleon's ambitions, crippling the French fleet in a four-day running battle known ever since as the Glorious First of June, and annihilating what was left of it at Trafalgar in 1804. In the words of the American naval strategist Admiral Alfred Mahan: "Those far distant, storm-beaten ships, upon which the Grand Alliance never looked stood between it and the domination of the world."

Based at Halifax, the Royal Navy's North American Squadron kept Nova Scotia and the other Maritime Provinces safe from invasion. By the end of the war, it had captured twelve American warships and burned three others,

RIGHT: Perpetual War *was one of a number of anonymous pamphlets – this one, authored by a "New England Farmer," was in fact written by John Lowell – that appeared in New England, opposing the war with England. Unhappiness with the war in New England was so pervasive that a secessionist movement was created demanding an end to hostilities.* (MCGILL UNIVERSITY LIBRARIES)

OPPOSITE PAGE: *James Madison's decision to declare war on Great Britain and to continue in spite of negotiations would prove costly to the United States and after lead to divisiveness after several failed military attacks.* (NATIONAL PORTRAIT GALLERY, SMITHSONIAN INSTITUTE)

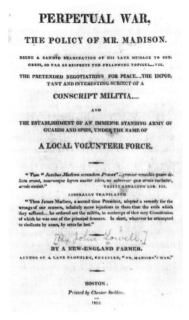

against a loss of six of its own vessels. In addition, it brought nearly five hundred captured American merchant ships into port. Privateers – Nova Scotia's main contribution to the war effort – captured another two hundred. Young men flocked to join the crews of swift fishing schooners, small brigs, and cutters that were fitted with a hodgepodge of armament to pursue the Americans. The most famous was the *Liverpool Packet* which ranged the New England coast, taking almost seventy merchantmen and earning more than $250,000 in prize money – an enormous sum at the time.

Privateering, also known as commerce raiding and *guerre de course*, made Halifax a wealthy city. Even before the war began, the seemingly interminable war with Napoleon had brought prosperity to Nova Scotia from military and naval contracts as well as French prizes. The war with the United States added to the province's wealth. "A constant bustle existed in our chief streets," a resident remembered. "Cannon were forever noisy. It was the salute of a man-of-war entering or leaving, practicing with the guns, or celebrating something or somebody."

On June 6, 1814, Haligonians celebrated the arrival of the frigates *Shannon* and *Chesapeake* after their deadly encounter off Boston in which the USS *Chesapeake*, now a mastless hulk, had struck her colours, despite her dying captain's injunction: "Don't give up the ship!"

A composite view showing USS Chesapeake *devastated by HMS Shannon's precisely aimed broadside, but with British colours already flying over the American frigate. The* Shannon's *captain, Philip Broke, was severely wounded in the fight. James Lawrence, the* Chesapeake's *commander, was killed but not before crying out, "Don't give up the ship!" It was a slogan that Commodore Oliver Perry would fly on a flag atop his mast at Put-In-Bay in September 1813.* (U.S. NAVAL ACADEMY MUSEUM)

Every housetop and every wharf was crowded with exited people as the ships entered the harbour. News of their arrival on Whitsunday morning had spread quickly throughout the city. Seventeen-year-old Thomas Chandler Haliburton, who would achieve fame as a humorist, recalls that word was passed from pew to pew in St. Paul's Church. The church soon emptied. Rowing to the *Chesapeake* with friends, he later described what he saw:

"Internally the scene was never to be forgotten by a landsman. The deck had not been cleaned, and the coils and folds of rope were steeped in gore as if in a slaughterhouse. She was a fir-build ship and her splinters had wounded nearly as many men as the *Shannon*'s shot. Pieces of skin with pendant hair were adhering to the sides of the ship, and in one place I saw portions of fingers protruding. Altogether it was a scene of devastation as difficult to forget as to describe. It is one of the most painful reminiscences of my youth."

Sailors carried the wounded to the Royal Naval Hospital, while the uninjured were taken to the military prison on Melville Island – one of the earliest prisons built by the British specifically to handle prisoners of war. The General Entry Book lists 8148 prisoners held here during the course of the war. Some were taken at battles on the Niagara frontier, but most were seamen, including the crews of at least forty privateers and merchantmen, as well as the crews of several warships, such as the *Chesapeake*. More than two hundred would die of typhus, smallpox, dysentery, and pneumonia.

On August 10, the American brig *Henry* of Salem, arrived in Halifax under a flag of truce to retrieve the bodies of the *Chesapeake*'s captain,

A British cartoon of the capturing of Chesapeake, *commanded by Captain James Lawrence who died of his wounds shortly after she struck her colours. The American frigate was taken as a prize of war into Halifax harbour.* (BROWN UNIVERSITY LIBRARY)

James Lawrence, and his first mate, Augustus Ludlow. They were buried in Trinity Church yard at the lower end of Broadway, after a solemn procession watched by 30,000 New Yorkers.

Word of the *Shannon*'s victory was greeted with jubilation in Britain and her captain, the generously named Philip Bowes Vere Broke, returned home to a hero's welcome. The name *Shannon* eventually passed to a new ship, whose naval brigade served with distinction during the Indian Mutiny of 1857-58. One of her crew, Able Seaman William Hall from Hantsport, Nova Scotia, won the Victoria Cross at the Relief of Lucknow, becoming the first black, the first Nova Scotian, and the third Canadian to receive this prestigious decoration. His parents were among the hundreds of escaped slaves from southern plantations the British conveyed to safety in 1814.

The Halifax squadron's blockade of the American coast was challenged by the American 44-gun super-frigates, the *United States, Constitution,* and *President,* each as powerful as a ship-of-the-line and faster than any British frigate. *Constitution,* or *Old Ironsides* as she was fondly known, easily bested HMS *Guerrière* off Sable Island on August 19, 1812. The *United States* and *President* were equally successful in single-ship actions. *Shannon*'s victory, then, was celebrated as it reasserted British supremacy at sea.

The end of the war in Europe also freed up Royal Navy warships and they were soon put to good use in North American waters. Vice Admiral Sir Alexander Cochrane, who was appointed commander at Halifax in March 1814, favoured a much more aggressive policy than that of his predecessor, directing his naval forces "to destroy and lay waste such towns and districts as you may find assailable." On August 3, he landed three of Wellington's battle-hardened regiments under the command of Major General Robert Ross, at Benedict, Maryland. Marching inland and determined to give the Americans "a complete drubbing before peace is made," Ross and his men burned Washington, then moved on to Baltimore. Struck down by a sniper's bullet near Fort McHenry, as a poetic young lawyer named Francis Scott Key watched "the bombs bursting in air, the "rocket's red glare," and the Stars and Stripes flying "by the dawn's early light," he was buried with full military honours in the Old Burying Ground in Halifax.

Like their practical New England neighbours, Maritimers had no appetite for the war, fearing that it would disrupt their lucrative seaborne trade. To prevent this, the Lieutenant Governor of Nova Scotia, Sir John Coape Sherbrooke, essentially established a truce with the New England states within days of the American declaration of war. On July 3, 1812, with the blessing of his Majesty's Council – most of its members drawn from Halifax's merchant elite – he issued a proclamation ordering all the King's subjects to abstain from attacking unarmed American vessels. Within months, a system of trading licenses was in place, allowing New England ships to enter Halifax or Saint John harbours at any time to trade certain specified articles. Occasionally, American merchants would arrange to have their ships seized by the British and taken to these ports, where, under the pretence of ransoming their vessels, the owners were paid for their cargoes. The system kept both sides happy.

Had it not been for American provisions, the British would have had great difficulty in simultaneously carrying on the wars against France and the United States. These provisions were shipped through Halifax to Wellington's armies in Spain and Portugal, to British soldiers in Upper and Lower Canada, Newfoundland, and to Nova Scotia itself for the civilian population and the Royal Navy. American merchants even ended up supplying the British fleet that blockaded their own coast and burned Washington. In the same way, British goods from the United Kingdom, Ireland, and West Indies were delivered to the United States. For nearly three years, Halifax served as a clearinghouse for much of North America's commerce.

As York, Newark, and Washington burned, Halifax reached its peak of prosperity. Soldiers and sailors reeled about the city's streets on drunken sprees at all hours of the day and night. A young Haligonian recalled:

"The upper streets were full of brothels; grog-shops and dancing houses were to be seen in almost every part of town. A portion of Grafton Street was known under the appellation of Hogg Street from a house of ill fame kept by a person of that name. The upper street along the base of Citadel Hill between the north and south barracks was known as 'Knock Him Down Street' in consequence of the number of affrays and even murders committed there. No person of any character ventured to reside there, nearly all the buildings being occupied as brothels for the soldiers and sailors. The streets of this part of town presented continually the disgusting sight of abandoned females of the lowest class in a state of drunkenness, bare headed, without shoes, and in the most filthy and abominable condition."

These and other areas, such as the "Beach" (Lower Water Street) – where fighting between the navy's press gangs and townsmen was almost a daily occurrence – co-existed with the splendid mansions of nearby Argyle and Barrington Streets. Yet, despite the city's prosperity, the great leveler, small-pox, struck during the winter of 1814-15, and hundreds of civilians and military personnel died – rich and poor alike.

There was no support for the war in New England, where it was dubbed "Mr. Madison's War." It was particularly unpopular in Massachusetts, where a secessionist movement had thrived before the war. The war itself only added to the disenchantment. Things came to a head in 1814 when representatives from all six New England states (Maine did not achieve statehood until 1820) met in secret in Hartford, Connecticut, and passed a series of resolutions against conscription and Congress's commercial regulations. Only the signing of the Treaty of Ghent forestalled New England's leaving the Union.

Although neither New Englanders nor Maritimers wanted the war, Sherbrooke's truce ended in 1814. Well aware of separatist feelings in New England, the New Brunswick Legislature, backed by the British government, moved to reclaim disputed territory along the international boundary. Sherbrooke was ordered to occupy that part of Maine "which at present intercepts the communication between Halifax and Quebec," leaving the details up to him. On the morning of September 1, 1814, he landed a force at Castine, Maine, at the mouth of the Penobscot River. What came to be known as the "Castine Expedition" was the only operation of the entire war that had the objective of occupying and holding American territory.

Moving upriver, the British occupied Hampden after a brief and relatively bloodless battle. The most formidable opposition came from Mrs. Martin Kinsley, the wife of the local magistrate. When British officers attempted to take over her home for use as a headquarters, Mrs. Kinsley, offended by their rudeness, took action. According to the Hampden Historical Society, "Mrs. Kinsley finally having her fill of the British, who might be officers but not gentlemen, ordered the hired girls to open the windows, and taking accurate aim, dumped the contents of the chamber pots on their heads. The stunned officers, their uniforms dripping, immediately left the property. Needless to say, neither Mrs. Kinsley nor the premises were bothered again during the British stay in Hampden. Before leaving, one officer was heard to remark, "If the militia had Mrs. Kinsley in command, Hampden would have been celebrating a victory instead of a defeat."

Bangor fell two days later, the residents venting their anger not so much upon the British but upon the local militia commander, General John Blake, for his poor showing, which they equated with treason. His effigy was shot, hanged, and burned. A court of inquiry after the war acquitted him of all charges, a decision that was based on the inferior forces at his disposal.

The British occupied Maine for eight months. Then, outmanoeuvred diplomatically by their American counterparts who were far more successful at the bargaining table than on the battlefield, they agreed to return the territory to the United States under the terms of the Treaty of Ghent, signed on Christmas Eve 1814. By the time they withdrew, they had collected almost £11,000 in customs duties. This so-called "Castine Fund" was used to finance Dalhousie University and the Cambridge Military Library in Halifax's Royal Artillery Park.

More than a century later, another lieutenant general unveiled a plaque honouring Sherbrooke's part in the founding of the library. Invitations to the ceremony were sent to the residents of Castine. None chose to attend.

OPPOSITE PAGE: *The capture of the* Cuyahoga Packet *off Fort Malden, with General William Hull's private documents aboard, provided General Isaac Brock with invaluable information about Detroit's defences. (PAINTING BY PETER RINDLISBACHER, FROM THE WAR OF 1812)*

ᔧ TO RULE THE WAVES

Compared with saltwater actions, naval battles on the Great Lakes were relatively minor, but the fighting was fierce and the outcome vital to both sides.

WHILE MUCH HAS BEEN written of the exploits of Brock, Sheaffe, Procter, de Salaberry, and other redoubtable military leaders in the War of 1812, we should not overlook the importance of the naval side.

Roads were few, of poor quality and vulnerable to seizure by the enemy and the blocking of supply routes. Waterways provided vital supply lines for the half-year or so when they were not frozen and both sides sought command of the lakes and rivers.

In the early days, naval warfare was very much a hit and miss affair. The Royal Navy was occupied with its role on the high seas, against both the United States and Napoleon's forces. As a result, it fell upon a somewhat hodgepodge organization, the Provincial Marine, to counter the United States' vessels on the lakes. While the latter were manned in large part by professional seamen, Provincial Marine crews were often brought up to strength by draftees and untrained soldiers. Founded over 30 years earlier, the service doubled as a merchant navy since its vessels had the monopoly on transportation on the Great Lakes. As they usually sailed only in daylight and within sight of land, high standards of seamanship were not expected. Some vessels were commanded by Royal Navy officers, who were seconded to the Marines as an alternative to layoffs on half pay.

Despite appeals by Sir George Prevost, Canada's Commander-in-Chief, for support from the Royal Navy, all that he received were a few officers and a handful of ratings. Indeed, the Lords of the Admiralty were so far out of touch that they went to great expense to send over a supply of water barrels, oblivious to the fact that the recipients had an unlimited supply of fresh water all around them.

In contrast, the Americans were well aware of the importance of the lakes. Operational plans for lakes Erie, Ontario and Champlain were prepared, and a group of sailors and craftsmen established a shipyard in Sackets Harbor, New York, in anticipation of hostilities.

First blood fell to the British. On July 2, 1812, a party from HMS *Hunter* commanded by a Trafalgar veteran, Quebecker Lieutenant Frederic Rolette, boarded and seized the U.S. schooner *Cuyahoga Packet* in Lake Erie, capturing not only the vessel, its cargo and a body of U.S. soldiers, but also the detailed plans and organization of General William Hull's opposing forces. Surprise was on Rolette's side, as the Americans were unaware that war had been officially declared. U.S. Lieutenant Woolsey seized a trio of Canadian schooners on Lake Ontario under similar circumstances and generated cries of "dirty pool."

This success was quickly followed by one of many combined operations which were to take place in the Great Lakes area. On July 16, army Captain Charles Roberts and a mixed force of about 600 regulars, militia, and Indians embarked in a fleet of canoes, bateaux, and the North West Company's armed schooner *Caledonia* to capture, without a shot, the strategically important Mackinac Island on the strait between lakes Michigan and Huron.

Soon, a number of new participants arrived to make their mark in the conflict. Sir James Yeo had just been acquitted by a West Indies courtmartial (he lost his ship on a reef) and was conveniently on hand to take charge of the naval forces. One notable subordinate was Commander Robert Barclay, a veteran explorer of the Pacific Coast who later lost an arm at Trafalgar. Barclay was despatched to Amherstburg, on Lake Erie, to command a force of five small ships and a larger vessel, HMS *Detroit*, which was still under construction. (A previous *Detroit*, the USS *Adams* captured and renamed, was in turn taken and destroyed in a daring small boat raid under U.S. Navy Lieutenant Jesse Elliott.)

The Americans appointed Captain Isaac Chauncey to the Great Lakes command. A veteran of the Tripoli campaign in 1804, he quickly organized the Sackets Harbor base as a productive shipyard. The gallant Elliott, having fallen afoul of U.S. President James Madison, was superseded in command in Lake Erie by an officer who, like Yeo, had recently been court-martialled and acquitted after running his vessel aground. Captain Oliver Hazard Perry, the new commander, accelerated the construction program at Presque Isle (now Erie, Pennsylvania) in a desperate production race with Barclay's force.

Frantic shipbuilding also took place on Lake Ontario. The Sackets Harbor yard competed with Canadian builders at York and Kingston. Hostilities took the form of sporadic sorties rather than pitched battles, as neither commander was willing to risk his ships in a major action.

Early in the war the whole Canadian fleet attacked Sackets Harbor, but despite weak opposition, quickly withdrew. One account has it that the Americans were short of ammunition, and local farmers gathered up the Canadian cannonballs, which their gunners fired back at the attackers.

Chauncey ventured forth in USS *General Pike* in an abortive raid on Burlington, Ontario, which ended in a minor pillaging expedition to York, but generally both commanders were content to live and let live.

When, on August 7, 1813, the two opposing squadrons finally met, the battle went to the British, mainly because two of Chauncey's largest vessels capsized in a sudden squall. Meanwhile, the naval spotlight moved to Commodore Perry on Lake Erie.

Despite a host of logistical difficulties, Perry's workers were able to build two large brigs and seven smaller vessels, with a total of 55 guns. Barclay had only six ships under his command, including *Detroit*, which was not yet fully equipped. The shallow waters of Lake Erie provided one advantage to

The American sloop of war General Pike *prepares to engage Sir James Yeo and HMS* Wolfe *on Lake Ontario on September 28, 1813.* (ENGRAVED BY R. RAWDON, U.S. NAVAL ACADEMY MUSEUM)

the Canadians: Perry's two major vessels drew too much water to cross the sandbank at the entrance to Presque Isle, and Barclay was able to blockade the port.

For some reason (rumour has it that Barclay had pulled his fleet back to the Canadian side of the lake to visit a young and attractive widow) the Canadian squadron left its post for five days. During that period, Perry was able to float his two largest vessels, USS *Lawrence* and *Niagara* over the sandbar and assemble his fleet at Put-in-Bay, to the west. To inspire his crews, his flagship *Lawrence* flew a pennant inscribed with the last words of its namesake, who had been defeated in *Chesapeake* earlier: "Don't Give Up The Ship."

Urged into action by his military commander, General Henry Procter, Commander Barclay reluctantly sailed to meet the foe. His vessels were outnumbered nine to six, and only a tenth of his crews were experienced seamen while about 60 per cent of Perry's larger complement were old salts. Barclay's only advantage lay in the number of guns, but his 65 pieces had a high proportion of long-range weapons, with lighter projectiles, as opposed to the heavier short-range carronades of the American ships. Worse, his flagship *Detroit* had been hastily equipped with a mixture of cannon from shore batteries, and he had few trained gunners.

The three-hour battle began at noon on September 10, 1813. First blood went to the British. Before the American vessels were able to close in and make use of their deadly carronades, the long guns from *Detroit* and *Queen Charlotte* battered Perry's flagship. Taking his "Don't Give Up The Ship"

Commodore Oliver Hazard Perry shifts his flag from the Niagara *at the height of the battle in this dramatized version of the event.*
(OHIO HISTORICAL SOCIETY)

pennant with him, he transferred his flag to *Niagara* while Lawrence struck her colours.

The British vessels were also badly damaged and Barclay was severely wounded. As *Niagara* closed in, the two major British ships collided and were unable to manoeuvre. It was the beginning of the end. A combination of grapeshot from the carronades and hot fire from the Kentucky riflemen who had volunteered to serve as marines soon forced the surrender of the British vessels. None of the six British vessels escaped. Lake Erie belonged to Perry and his fleet. The fledgling U.S. Navy now had a new slogan: "We have met the enemy and they are ours." (To add to his laurels, Perry joined General William Henry Harrison in his foray into Canada and led an infantry charge at the battle of the Thames the following month.)

Meanwhile, on Lake Ontario, Chauncey's fleet met a smaller group of Admiral Yeo's vessels, damaging two of them. Yeo fled for the safety of Burlington harbour, but, surprisingly, Chauncey failed to follow up on his advantage and withdrew, consoling himself with the capture of five small schooners. After the thaw of 1814, Yeo (who had gained a lead in the shipbuilding race and now ruled the lake) attacked Oswego in a combined operation, seizing a quantity of much-needed supplies, and later blockaded Sackets Harbor. From then on the naval commanders appeared content to engage in building bigger and better ships, none of which saw action.

When Admiral Yeo assumed command at Lake Ontario he replaced some of the naval officers already there. One, Captain Daniel Pring, was relegated to the command of a trio of barges, each mounting a single gun at

Île aux Noix, which guarded the entrance to the Richelieu River from Lake Champlain.

In June 1813, two American warships on Lake Champlain tested the British defences. It was a fatal error. Caught in the Richelieu, the vessels were unable to turn and use their 11-gun broadsides, while the nippy British gunboats battered the enemy hulls at water level. Under fire from the Île aux Noix garrison and Pring's boats, the Americans were forced to surrender. A month later those captured sloops, now flying the British ensign, along with Pring's gunboats, ruled Lake Champlain and removed any threat of U.S. plans to advance on Montreal.

A shipbuilding race had begun and, by September 1814, each side had one major vessel, three smaller warships and about a dozen gunboats (crewed by oarsmen and mounting one or two cannon) on Lake Champlain. The procrastinating Sir George Prevost finally decided that he could no longer put off an invasion through the Lake Champlain-Lake George corridor. This was to be a combined operation.

The beginning was inauspicious. Admiral Yeo sent Captain George Downie to take over command from Pring, now relegated to second-in-command of the naval force. Downie had never seen Lake Champlain before. While the forces were equal, once again the Royal Navy relied on its long guns, the Americans on their carronades. Downie experienced Barclay's problems from the previous year. His flagship *Confiance* was rushed from the shipyard before completion. Her guns having neither been zeroed nor fired, and with a crew of civilian carpenters still aboard working on final touches, the vessel led the tiny fleet into action.

Battle began at 0800 hrs on September 11. The American vessels, with Commander Thomas MacDonough commanding in USS *Saratoga*, were anchored in line off Plattsburg Bay. Although *Confiance*'s opening broadside severely damaged *Saratoga*, two volleys from the American vessel badly disabled the British flagship, killing Downie. A murderous exchange of carronade fire took place between the two major vessels. MacDonough had prudently arranged for his ships to be anchored so that they could be swung around on the cables while the British ships depended on the capricious wind to manoeuvre. This proved to be a decisive factor, for when MacDonough's starboard batteries were disabled, he was able to swing his vessel and bring his port broadside to bear. By noon the battle was over. The last British vessel to strike her flag was the brig *Linnet*, commanded by the redoubtable Lieutenant Pring, who fought on alone for a quarter hour after the other vessels had surrendered. The gunboats, which had served him so well earlier, lacked his aggressive spirit. Seven of them did not even enter the arena; while the remaining five stayed well clear of the battle, as their commander had left them to take refuge in a hospital vessel.

After MacDonough's victory, Sir George Prevost, unable to control the vital supply route on the lakes, returned to Montreal with his tail between his legs. While he blamed the navy for its failure, Admiral Yeo was even more ready to place the blame on the army, as the American ships were well within range of the land-based artillery, which took no part in the action.

The final significant action on the Great Lakes took place in the Strait of Mackinac, the entrance to Lake Huron. Here two American schooners, which had hitherto enjoyed a free hand on the lake (sinking HMS *Nancy*, a supply vessel) were captured in a daring small boat operation, leaving the British in command of the lake.

Compared with the saltwater actions, the lake battles were relatively minor. The total guns employed by both sides in the Lake Erie or Lake Champlain battles numbered less than the armament of a single ship of the line. Nevertheless, the fighting was fierce. As one veteran declared, "compared with Lake Champlain, Trafalgar was child's play." Both sides achieved strategic gains, and, by the war's end in 1815, the British owned lakes Huron and Ontario while the United States controlled Erie and Champlain.

Perhaps the unsung heroes of the battle for the lakes were the shipwrights and workers of Presque Isle, Sackets Harbor, Kingston, York and St. Jean who toiled under atrocious conditions, improvised to compensate for the lack of vital materials and were constantly vulnerable to enemy attack. Without their efforts the fighting captains could have done nothing. Theirs is a story in itself.

❧ THE LEGACY

*The War of 1812 left an indelible mark
on Canada. Its legacy is the world's
longest undefended border.*

"HOW UNCOMFORTABLY LIKE a civil war it seemed," John
Le Couteur of the 104th Foot wrote in the autumn of 1813. "Colonels
Cutting and Preston, Majors Malcolm, Cummings and Johnston, Captains
Jones, Christie and Chapman. Strange indeed did it appear to me to find so
many familiar names as enemies – the very names of Officers in our own
Army."

The enthusiastic young officer had sailed into Halifax to join his regiment on the "balmy, soft evening" of June 21, 1812, unaware that the
United States had declared war on Great Britain three days before. In years
to come, he would fight in six major engagements and countless skirmishes,
suffer sickness and short rations, and endure an epic winter march from
Fredericton to Kingston. In January 1815, older and wiser, he would re-
joice at "the blessed news of Peace" and "the close of a hot and unnatural

RIGHT: "The Signing of the Treaty of Ghent, Christmas Eve, 1814." Painting by Sir Amedee Forestier. (NATIONAL COLLECTION OF FINE ARTS, SMITHSONIAN INSTITUTION)

OPPOSITE PAGE: By 1814, both the British and Americans were operating navies on Lake Ontario of a size and strength inconceivable in 1812. The 1816 Rush-Bagot Agreement would limit the number of warships allowed on the Lakes. ("LAKE ONTARIO PATROL, 1814" BY PETER RINDLISBACHER)

war between kindred people."

There is a story that the man who fired the first shot across the river at Detroit killed his best friend on the American side. A plausible story, as almost everyone in this "unnatural war" had a friend or relative on the other side. General Roger Sheaffe had a sister in Boston, William Hull a brother living on the Thames.

It was a war that almost no one wanted. The British, at war with Napoleon on the continent, tried to prevent it, but when they could not, saw it as more a troublesome sideshow. Canadians, preoccupied with carving homes out of the wilderness, did not want it, nor did New Englanders, who largely sat it out. Nova Scotia issued a proclamation announcing that the province would "abstain from predatory warfare against our neighbours" and that trade would continue as usual. "Congress," an American editor said, "was driven, goaded, dragged, forced, and kicked into the conflict by that small group which Thomas Jefferson called the War Hawks."

Apart from the War Hawks, only Tecumseh and his followers welcomed the war, seizing the opportunity it presented to reclaim the lands they had lost to American settlers in the northwest. Abandoned and betrayed, they were the war's great losers. But some had a very good war: prices rose and profits soared; farmers prospered while workers were in demand to build forts, barracks and ships; Americans on the eastern shore of Lake Champlain fed British and Canadian troops fighting on the western side; and merchants in Montreal grew rich trading with the New England states. By 1814, three quarters of the beef consumed in Canada was supplied by

American contractors. Increased trade along the St. Lawrence and Great Lakes stimulated the building of canals and railways in the post-war years.

Veterans of the war rose to prominent positions in American public life. Three – William Henry Harrison, Andrew Jackson, and Zachary Taylor – became president. In Canada, Isaac Brock and Laura Secord were hailed as national heroes, while Bishop Strachan, William Allan, and John Beverley Robinson emerged as charter members of the Family Compact. Anti-American, elitist and of proven loyalty to the Crown, they would resist any movement for reform and sow the seeds for the Rebellion of 1837 in Upper Canada.

As in all wars, however, the vast majority suffered: 8774 British and Canadian soldiers lost their lives as did 7738 Americans and thousands more were wounded. Aggravated by poor harvests in 1812 and 1814, food shortages plagued the Niagara Peninsula and the area west of the Grand River. Towns and villages on both sides of the border were put to the torch.

An American, travelling from Buffalo, New York, to Detroit, Michigan, in 1816, wrote: "I was most sensibly struck with the devastation which had been made by the late war, farms formerly in high cultivation, now laid waste; houses entirely evacuated and forsaken; provisions of all kinds very scare; and where peace and plenty abounded, poverty and destruction now stalked over the land."

Negotiations to end the war began almost as soon as it started. When it became obvious that the conquest of Canada would involve more than marching, the Americans accepted a Russian proposal to mediate an end to the conflict. Delegates were dispatched to St. Petersburg in March 1813 with instructions to impress upon the British "the advantage to both countries promised by a transfer of the upper parts and even the whole of Canada to the United States." To do so, the Americans argued, would remove "a fruitful source of controversy" and relieve Great Britain of the burden of supporting Canada "which must be considerable in peace or war, especially in war."

As the British had no intention of ceding Canada, the talks collapsed. Direct negotiations began in the summer of 1814 at Ghent, the ancient capital of Flanders, with three principal subjects for discussion on the agenda: the impressment of American seamen into the Royal Navy, the establishment

TOP: *Between 1756 and 1815 British North American ships were allowed, indeed encouraged, to attack and seize enemy ships or those trading with the enemy. In order not to be treated as pirates, privateers received a marque (license) from the governor. Hundreds of ships from New England to the Carribbean harassed French, Dutch, Spanish, and American vessels. Depicted here is the privateer* Rover *from Liverpool, Nova Scotia, engaging the Spanish schooner* Santa Rita *on September 10, 1800 off the Venuzuelan coast. (ILLUSTRATION BY TOM BJARNASON, READERS DIGEST)*

ABOVE: *The hostility of the Americans toward Indians pushed them to form alliances with the British. The Indian warrior was much feared by American colonists on the frontiers and the British took advantage of these fears both on the field of battle and as propaganda to intimidate the Americans. (PAINTING BY JOHN MIX STANLEY, NATIONAL MUSEUM OF AMERICAN ART, SMITHSONIAN INSTITUTE)*

LEFT: Sir Isaac Brock helped Canada hold out against the Americans in the early part of the war. He would die leading an infantry assault against the Americans at Queenston Heights on October 13, 1812. (PORTRAIT BY J.W.L. FORESTER, NAC/C-7760)

ABOVE: General Isaac Brock's success over the American forces at Queenston and their subsequent withdrawal back across the Niagara River was a pivotal point early in the war. British regulars, Canadian militia and warriors from the Six Nations defeated 2000 American militiamen on October 13, 1812 at the Battle of Queenston Heights. Shot by an American sharpshooter, Brock died almost instantly. With the arrival of fresh British troops, the Americans would call a retreat. Brock's monument, forever immortalizing the beloved leader, commemorates the British victory at Queenston Heights. (NAC/C-273)

ABOVE: *A composite view showing* Chesapeake *at the moment she was devastated by* Shannon's *precisely aimed broadside, but with British colours flying already over the American. Philip Broke was severely wounded in the fight, and James Lawrence was killed, but not before crying out, "Don't give up the ship!", a slogan that Commodore Oliver Hazard Perry would fly on a flag at Put-In Bay in September of the same year, 1813.* (U.S. NAVAL ACADEMY MUSEUM)

RIGHT: *James Madison's decision to declare war on Great Britain and to continue in spite of negotiations would prove costly to the United States and lead to divisiveness, particularly in the New England states, after several failed military attacks.* (NATIONAL PORTRAIT GALLERY, SMITHSONIAN INSTITUTE)

ABOVE: On June 22, 1813, Laura Secord made her way through difficult terrain from Queenston to warn James FitzGibbon at Beaver Dams, of the approaching American forces and of the impending attack on his post. In this romantic image, the dishevelled heroine is ushered into FitzGibbon's office by a British soldier and a Mohawk warrior. ("MRS. SECORD WARNING FITZGIBBON" BY LORNE K. SMITH, PUBLIC ARCHIVES OF CANADA) **ABOVE RIGHT:** American infantry officer, northern campaign of 1813. Possibly an officer of the New York State militia, some of whom did cross into Canada with Hampton. (PARKS CANADA) **FAR LEFT:** An American infantryman of the 1813 campaign, as he might have appeared at Châteauguay as part of Wade Hampton's army. By October, the thin summer uniforms would be threadbare, and both at Châteauguay and on the St. Lawrence the American troops suffered severly from exposure. (PARKS CANADA) **MIDDLE LEFT:** An enlisted man of the United States army artillery, which was present at Châteauguay and at Crysler's Farm in 1813. The artilleryman would sling his musket while serving as a member of a gun crew. (PARKS CANADA) **LEFT:** The 2nd Regiment of United States Light Dragoons, cavalry who would dismount and fight as infantry, were the advance scouts for Hampton's army as it approached the Châteauguay and de Salaberry's waiting force. (PARKS CANADA)

ABOVE: *On October 26, 1813, Lieutenant Colonel Charles-Michel de Salaberry built a defensive position at a bend in the Châteauguay River. His troops, the Voltigeurs Canadiens, handily defeated a force four times their size, in effect saving Montreal and Lower Canada from American control.* ("THE BATTLE OF CHÂTEAUGUAY" BY H. DE HOLMFELD, CHÂTEAU DE RAMEZAY).

OPPOSITE TOP: *General Henry Procter's British infantry were cut down by the skilled mounted Kentuckians at Moraviantown on October 5, 1813. Led by Richard Johnson, the battle lasted only minutes as the thundering American cavalry, armed with tomahawks, flintlock pistols and muskets, shattered the loosely-formed British line. Procter withdrew to avoid capture, leaving his troops to their fate as the infantry broke and fled. Meanwhile, another American column descended on the position held by Tecumseh and his warriors. The Shawnee chief's death would lead to the end of Indian resistance south of the Great Lakes.* (KEN RILEY, NATIONAL GUARD HERITAGE).

OPPOSITE LEFT: *After he failed to take Fort Meigs on July 26, 1813, Procter, following the advice of Tecumseh, ordered the attack on the small American post of Fort Stephenson. The American fort was commanded by Major George Groghan and defended by just 160 regular infantry and one six-pounder gun. The stockade surrounding the fort remained intact after several hours of bombardment from Procter's field guns and mortars. Groghan ordered his men to hold their fire until the advancing British 41st Regiment was less than 100 feet away. Scores fell as the Americans fired volley after volley from the safety of their compound. Unable to climb over or hack their way through the palisade, Procter was forced to retreat when he received word of approaching American forces. The failure would cost the British over 100 dead and add to the growing list of Procter's failings.* ("ATTACK ON FORT STEPHENSON" BY J.C.H. FORSTER, FORT MALDEN NATIONAL HISTORICAL SITE)

RIGHT: *Thomas Jefferson's belief that the conquest of Canada would be a "mere matter of marching" led the U.S. close to disaster.* (PORTRAIT BY CHARLES WILLSON PEALE, INDEPENDANCE NATIONAL HISTORIC PARK)

LEFT: The hard-fought battle of Lundy's Lane cost the British and Americans dearly. The bloodiest one-day battle of the war occurred on July 25, 1814 and, although the American commander, General Jacob Brown, claimed victory, he withdrew his forces to the safety of Fort Erie, discarding baggage along the way. ("BATTLE OF LUNDY'S LANE, BRITISH DEFENDING COMMONS WITH BAYONETS" BY C.W. JEFFERYS, CITY OF TORONTO ARCHIVES)

BOTTOM LEFT: Detail of a mural by Adam Sherriff Scott of the Battle at Crysler's Farm, where Lieutenant-Colonel Joseph Morrison fought a classic set-piece battle against the Americans. His victory on November 11, 1813 resounded throughout the Canadas. The Kingston Gazette praised Morrison's troops for having "displayed the true spirit of British soldiers." (ST. LAWRENCE PARKS COMMISSION)

BOTTOM RIGHT: The ghastly effects of cannon fire and the impact of heavy lead musket balls were captured in Napoleonic-era drawings by British army physician Charles Bell. Men suffering wounds of this nature as often died of shock as from the gangrene and infection that invariably set in. (ROYAL ARMY MEDICAL CORPS MUSEUM, LONDON, ENGLAND)

LEFT: *Believing he would be facing ill-trained militia, British General Phineas Riall cried out, "Those are regulars, by God!" at the sight of his enemy. "The morning light ushered…a shocking spectacle. Men and horses lying promiscuously together, Americans and English, laid upon one another," wrote Sergeant Commins of the Battle of Chippewa.* (PAINTING BY H. CHARLES MCBARREN, U.S. ARMY CENTRE OF MILITARY HIST.)

BOTTOM LEFT: *Robert Barclay's Lake Erie squadron makes ready for departure from Amherstburg naval station, September 7, 1813. Barclay would sail his flagship HMS Detroit to the Bass Islands to confront American Commodore Oliver Perry at his anchorage at Put-In Bay. The battle was a disaster for the Royal Navy and the Canadians. On September 12, Perry wrote: "We have met the enemy and they are ours; two ships, two brigs, one schooner and one sloop." (PAINTING BY PETER RINDLISHBACHER)*

BELOW: *The man on the left had been blinded by a musket ball that passed through both his eyes; the man on the right had his cheek peirced by a ball. It was the American custom to load muskets with smaller "buckshot" as well as ball, to make them more lethal. (ROYAL ARMY MEDICAL CORPS MUSEUM, LONDON, ENGLAND)*

ABOVE: *On June 19, 1816, almost by accident, Cuthbert Grant and his band of Métis, met a group of local settlers at Seven Oaks (now part of Winnipeg) on the Red River. Governor Robert Semple, with 27 men, marched from the settlement at the junction of the Red and Assiniboine Rivers (now central Winnipeg) to ascertain what was happening. Although no one was spoiling for a fight, a nervous settler grabbed a Métis' bridle, sparking the massacre of 21 settlers.* (GLENBOW - ALBERTA INSTITUTE)

LEFT: *William Napier was hired as an engineer on Hind's expedition to Red River. Trained as a topographical artist, he sketched a number of scenes while en route to Red River, as well as different winter activities around Fort Garry where he spent the winter of 1857-1858. In this watercolour, Napier depicts local Indians in their traditional clothing.* ("SAULTEAUX INDIANS, FORT GARRY CIRCA 1857-1858" BY WILLIAM NAPIER, NAC/C-146728)

TOP: *Thousands of men implicated in the Mackenzie Rebellion of December 1837 were hunted down by reward-seeking bounty hunters and British regulars. Many of them were beaten and treated cruelly by their captors. (PUBLIC ARCHIVES OF ONTARIO)*

ABOVE LEFT: *Thomas Conant was a casualty of the 1837 rebellion in Upper Canada, killed by a drunken dispatch rider outside his home north of Toronto. But in the eyes of the law, he was a rebel. During the soldier's trial, the testimony of witnesses was not admitted and he was found innocent. In the chaos of the rebellion, many personal feuds were settled. (PUBLIC ARCHIVES OF CANADA)*

ABOVE RIGHT: *During the uprising of November 1837, Patriotes seized the Ellice Manor at Beauharnois near Montreal. They waited for guns that never came and fled when confronted by 1500 Glengarry Highlanders from Upper Canada. (KATHERINE JANY ELLICE, PAC)*

ABOVE: With the Cariboo gold rush of 1858, a road was required to facilitate the trade generated by the population boom. In the spring of 1862, British Columbia's governor, James Douglas, ordered the construction of the Cariboo Road. Heading north from Yale, British Columbia, by 1865 the road went as far as Barkerville. Designed and surveyed by Royal Engineers, the road through the Fraser Valley was built primarily by Chinese labourers using picks and shovels. (PAINTING BY REX WOODS, MCCORD MUSEUM)

RIGHT: In 1858, gold was discovered in the Cariboo region of British Columbia. "Free miners" with picks, shovels and gold pans headed towards the Fraser River and the hope of El Dorado. By 1868, mines and stakes were being bought and sold by larger companies that could afford heavy machinery. The day of the Cariboo "free miner" was over, but only after taking millions of dollars of gold out of the ground in the most challenging terrain in Canada. (SELF PORTRAIT BY WILLIAM HIND)

TOP: The "Old Canadian Pacific Express." Hudson's Bay Company and Nor' Wester voyageurs worked 16 to 18 hours a day, paddling, always paddling. Despite its many perils, these hardy men found the life rewarding. (PUBLIC ARCHIVES OF CANADA) *ABOVE:* An idealized Colonel John By – he was actually rather short and stocky – at the headlocks of the Rideau Canal in 1826, from what is now Ottawa's Major's Hill Park. (PUBLIC ARCHIVES OF CANADA)

of a separate Indian state, and the revision of the 1783 boundary between the Canadas and the United States. Five months later, on Christmas Eve, the delegates affixed their signatures to six copies of a treaty that, in effect, changed nothing.

Both sides had recognized that the only way they could reach an agreement was to moderate their demands. The British dropped their insistence on an Indian nation and boundary changes that would have given Canada part of Maine, a strip of land along the east side of the Niagara River, and Michilimackinac. The Americans, however, were unanimous in their refusal to give up any territory. War weariness, Prevost's defeat at Plattsburg and the intervention of the Duke of Wellington broke the deadlock. "It is my opinion that the war has been a most successful one and highly honourable to British arms," the Duke told the prime minister, urging him "to make peace now."

The Treaty of Ghent was a triumph for American diplomacy. It said no more than that the situation that had prevailed before war was declared would continue under the general principle of the status quo *ante bellum*. Trade, fisheries, maritime grievances and boundary disputes – the very reasons for the war – were totally ignored. All conquered territory would be reciprocally restored "without delay, and without causing any destruction." Nothing was said about disarmament on the Great Lakes, and the Indians, whom the British had hoped to protect and reward for their services, were left to the mercy of the Americans.

The Rush-Bagot Agreement of 1816 later limited the number of warships allowed on the Great Lakes and the Webster-Ashburton Treaty of 1842 would finally settle outstanding border disputes. "The blessed news of peace," unfortunately, did not discourage the British from spending enormous sums on fortifications at Fort Henry, along the Rideau Canal, at Fort Lennox, and the citadels at Quebec and Halifax.

In due course, when Canada inherited responsibility for her own security and defence as well as the former British forts, common sense and the great disparity with the United States in men, money, and material dictated the need for friendly relations.

What became known and celebrated as "the longest undefended border in the world" made a virtue of necessity.

༄ MASSACRE AT SEVEN OAKS

After a brief standoff with the Métis, 21 settlers were dead, including Robert Semple, governor of the Red River settlement.

RIVALRY FOR THE CONTROL of the fur trade did not end with the fall of New France. On a smaller scale, the struggle for power and wealth continued unabated between the Hudson's Bay Company and the North West Company, a loosely-knit alliance of independent Scottish, French-Canadian, and Métis traders. This competition would culminate on June 19, 1816, in a murderous 15-minute fusillade at Seven Oaks, near the junction of the Red and Assiniboine rivers, in the heart of what is now Winnipeg.

The fur trade and exploration in western Canada had forged ahead since the La Vérendrye's epic journeys in the 1730s. In the wake of singular men like David Thompson, Hearn, and Alexander Mackenzie, a society slowly formed on the Prairies. As more fur trading posts were established, more

RIGHT: *Saulteaux Indians from the Upper Assiniboine River area, circa 1887. Members of the Saulteaux tribe helped the settlers when they came under attack from James Duncan Cameron's Métis.* (NAC/PA-050799)

OPPOSITE PAGE: *On June 19, 1816, Cuthbert Grant and his band of Métis met a group of local settlers at Seven Oaks on the Red River, which is now part of the city of Winnipeg. One thing led to another, and before they knew it, a massacre was underway.* (GLENBOW-ALBERTA INSTITUTE)

traders wintered with the natives and took native or "country" wives. And a new people was born: the Métis.

One of the traders was Daniel Harmon, who traveled west with the voyageurs in 1799 as a clerk with the North West Company. The trip was arduous, and the cultivated young New Englander did not care for the voyageurs' company. "They are great talkers but in the utmost sense of the word thoughtless," he wrote. "All of their chat is about horses, dogs, canoes and women, and strong men who can fight a good battle."

Harmon spent 19 years in trading posts across the west, married a Métis woman and fathered eleven children. His family spoke a mixture of Cree, French, and English and, like most Métis families, was entirely dependent upon the fur trade.

Settlement was the natural enemy of the fur trade. Sir Alexander Mackenzie, who had retired from the business but still defended the interests of the North West Company, attacked the very idea of settlement as preposterous. As someone who knew the area, he said he could attest that it was "never intended for man, but for raw nature." It was with consternation, then, that he learned that a wealthy Scottish aristocrat, Thomas Douglas, the fifth earl of Selkirk, planned to establish a colony in the Red River region known as Assiniboia.

In 1792, Selkirk had toured the Scottish Highlands, where tenants were being forced off the land to make room for sheep, which landlords found were far more profitable. It was an impoverished and dispirited place, and Selkirk became involved in the Highlanders' plight, writing a book, *Observations on the Present State of the Highlands of Scotland*, in which he argued that emigration was inevitable.

At his own expense, Selkirk undertook to settle as many Highlanders as possible in British North America, establishing colonies in Prince Edward Island and at Baldoon, near present day Chatham, Ontario. But these were only the prelude to his major undertaking in the very heart of Canada – the Red River Valley.

As a major shareholder in the Hudson's Bay Company, Selkirk persuaded the company to sell him 300,000 square kilometers of land, sprawling across what is now Manitoba, Saskatchewan, North Dakota, and Minnesota – an area five times the area of Scotland – for ten shillings. A successful agricultural colony, he argued, would not only give the Highlanders a new start, it would also provide the company with a secure food supply for its trading posts and serve as a bulwark against American encroachment.

In August 1812, Miles Macdonell, a hot-tempered former soldier whom Selkirk had recruited as governor of Assiniboia, embarked at Stornoway with 36 prospective settlers. Enduring a bitterly cold winter at York Factory, they did not reach the promised land until the following summer. Macdonell formally claimed possession by reading their charter to the few colonists with him – and the surrounding wilderness.

The Red River country was flood-prone and barren for most of the year. It was also a place where a dispossessed Highlander could make a new life for himself and his family on land that was wonderfully fertile. Problem was, the Nor'Westers, the French inhabitants, and the Métis also laid claim to the land, disputing the Hudson's Bay Company's right to give it away. This land served as the Nor'Westers' supply depot for food and furs and they viewed Selkirk's grand scheme as a plot to "become a monopolizer of the fur trade."

A second group of colonists arrived the following year, but settlement was difficult. The Red River flooded its banks, and the crops failed.

Macdonell soon made a bad situation worse. In January 1814, facing famine, he issued a proclamation declaring that "no persons trading furs or Provisions within the Territory shall take out any provisions, either of flesh or game or vegetables." What came to be known as the "Pemmican Proclamation," effectively banned the export of food from Red River, threatening the North West Company's ability to supply its trading posts. James

Duncan Cameron of the Nor'Westers predicted violence: "Macdonell is now determined not only to seize our pemmican, but to drive us out of the Assiniboia district and consequently out of the north west. Hostilities will no doubt begin early this spring."

Cameron rallied the Métis behind him. "You must assist me in driving away the colony," he told them. "If they are not driven away, the consequence will be that they will prevent you from hunting. They will starve your families, and they will put their feet in the neck of those that attempt to resist them. You can easily see how they mean to finish by what they have begun already." The Métis heeded his call.

"They immediately began to burn our houses in the day time and fire upon us during the night, saying the country was theirs," wrote John Pritchard, one of the settlers. "If we did not immediately quit the settlement, they would plunder our property, and burn the houses over our heads."

With the help of the Saulteaux Indians, the settlers retreated to Norway House, a Hudson's Bay Company trading post at the north end of Lake Winnipeg. The Nor'Westers also persuaded more than a hundred settlers to accept transportation and resettlement in Upper Canada. Macdonell, disillusioned and angry with Selkirk, was arrested for "stealing pemmican" on a warrant issued by a magistrate who was also an employee of the North West Company.

Later that year, the settlers returned to Red River to rebuild, with a new governor, Robert Semple. However, the resentment and determination of the Nor'Westers and Métis to stamp out the colony continued unabated.

On June 19, 1816, the skirmishes, arson, and terrorism culminated in a massacre at Seven Oaks, a clump of trees that skirted a ravine a mile from the Hudson's Bay Company's Red River trading post. That evening, Governor Semple had ridden out from the settlement to confront a group of Métis wearing war paint, who had earlier captured three settlers working in their fields. Ordering 28 men to follow him, Semple approached a Métis named François Boucher and asked him what he wanted. A tense standoff ensued, with the settlers facing a rough skirmish line of angry, mounted Métis. Words were exchanged and Semple reached out and grabbed the bridle of Boucher's horse. It was a foolish and fatal move.

As Boucher's horse reared and he fell to the ground, the Métis opened fire. Semple was the first to fall, hit in the thigh. The others, many of them wounded, milled about in confusion until another volley tore through their ranks. "In a few minutes, almost all our people were either killed or wounded," John Pritchard, one of the few surviving settlers, recalled. "Captain Rogers, having fallen, rose up again and came towards me... I called out to him, 'For God's sake give yourself up!' ... He raised up his hands and called out for mercy. A half-breed shot him through the head and another cut open his belly with a knife."

Semple, whose leg was broken, was spared by Cuthbert Grant, the leader of the Métis who had rushed forward to protect him from the fury of the others. When he attempted to prevent further bloodshed, one of his followers pushed him away and shot Semple dead. The wounded were dispatched with knife and tomahawk, their bodies hacked apart.

The outnumbered settlers had managed to fire several shots, killing one Métis and wounding another. But their casualties were appalling: 21 of 29 men were dead, and two wounded. The remaining settlers were spared, but their houses were pillaged and they again retreated to Norway House.

Lord Selkirk was in Upper Canada when he learned of the killings at Seven Oaks. Determined not to be intimidated by the Nor'Westers, he hired about 100 disbanded soldiers of the De Meurons Regiment that had been engaged as mercenaries during the War of 1812. Resolutely and with righteous indignation, he then proceeded to Fort William, the headquarters of the North West Company, and captured it. He had several officers of the company arrested and then moved on to Red River to restore his beloved colony. Alexander Ross, one of the original settlers, left this account of the De Meurons:

"They were chiefly foreigners, a medley of almost all nations – Germans, French, Italians, Swiss, and others; and, with few exceptions, were a rowdy and lawless set of black guards. These men had entered into written agreements with Lord Selkirk, and were to be paid at a certain rate per month... They were, further, to have lands assigned to them in the settlement, if they chose to remain; and otherwise, were to be conveyed, at his Lordship's expense, either to Montreal or Europe. As the event proved, they preferred the former, and were rewarded with small grants of land... The De Meurons were bad farmers, as all old soldiers generally are, and withal very bad subjects; quarrelsome, slothful, famous bottle companions, and ready for any enterprise, however lawless and tyrannical. Under any circumstances, a levy of this character could be no great acquisition to a new settlement and at such a juncture, as we have described should never have been permitted by the Canadian Government."

Meanwhile, the North West Company had a warrant issued for the arrest of Lord Selkirk. He ignored it and, instead, attempted to have those responsible for the massacre at Seven Oaks brought to trial. However, his efforts were unsuccessful, and Selkirk himself was fined 2000 pounds for his action against Fort William. Disillusioned and in ill health, he returned to Europe. He died in France in 1820 at the age of 48.

A year later, exhausted by the competition and violence, the North West Company and the Hudson's Bay Company did the unthinkable and agreed to join forces under the latter company's name.

Selkirk's unlikely settlement prospered. Thirty years after he described it as "gloomy as the Ultima Thule," Alexander Ross had this to say: "No farmers in the world, no settlement or colony of agriculturalists can be pronounced so happy, independent and comfortable as those in Red River."

Except for the Métis. As they had feared, the success of the Red River colony marked the end of the fur trade – and their livelihoods. Neglected and impoverished, seen as an impediment to future growth, many sold their lands and drifted away to the northwest. Those that remained would, in time, turn to another prophet: Louis Riel.

RIGHT: *Governor Robert Semple was killed at Seven Oaks.* (NAC)

FAR RIGHT: *Thomas Douglas, the Fifth Earl of Selkirk. In 1803 he settled 800 displaced Highlanders on land he purchased in PEI, and the following year established another settlement at Baldoon, Upper Canada. In 1811, he received a large land grant from the Hudson's Bay Company in what is now Manitoba, and established the Red River Colony in 1812, arriving to supervise it himself in 1815 before returning to Europe three years later.*

❧ UNREST IN THE CANADAS

John A. Macdonald's war.

IN THE SUMMER OF 1837, Kingston seemed blessed. In Britain the first great railway boom came to a sudden end, while in the United States a financial panic almost brought economic collapse. When American banks suspended credit and payments in specie, Canadian banks followed suit. Crops failed, the timber trade faltered and shipping in the St. Lawrence dwindled to a trickle. Flour had to be imported at ruinous prices. The streets of Montreal and towns and villages across Upper and Lower Canada took on a Sunday quiet. "In my day," wrote Peter McGill, president of the Bank of Montreal, "such times have never been experienced."

But Kingston flourished. The completion of the Rideau Canal, the construction of the great fortress at Fort Henry and the decision to build the provincial penitentiary at Portsmouth, all contributed to the town's prosperity and pointed to a bright future. On Quarry Street an ambitious young lawyer, hoping to share that future, established his first practice. "John A. Macdonald, Attorney," he announced in the Chronicle and Gazette, "has

RIGHT: Sir Francis Bond Head (1793-1875), governor of Upper Canada. Vain, posturing, and inflexible, he infuriated responsible Tories and Reformers alike. London recalled him in 1838. (PAC)

OPPOSITE PAGE: As a militia private, John A. Macdonald marched against the rebels, and later defended the accused in court. He would become Canada's first prime minister in 1867. (PAC/C-10144)

opened his office in the brick building belonging to Mr. Collar, opposite the shop of D. Prentiss Esq., where he will attend to all the duties of his profession."

Tall, congenial, with a rich store of anecdotes and "a smiling capacity for liquor," the homely young lawyer was soon a popular and busy man about town. He was elected president of the Kingston Young Men's Society in the autumn of 1837, informing the members that the first subject of debate in the winter program would be "Are the works of Nature sufficient in themselves to prove the existence of a Supreme Being?" No doubt they also discussed the worsening political situation.

The new governor of Upper Canada, Sir Francis Bond Head – a posturing, vainglorious man devoid of political experience and common sense – had within a few short months quarrelled with his Executive Council and the Reform Assembly, dissolved the House and appealed to the whole province to join him in the defence of British institutions against radical democracy and republicanism. Armed mobs were reported to be gathering north of Toronto. In Lower Canada, Patriotes were rumoured to have clashed with loyalists at Montréal and St. Charles. On November 3, the residents of Kingston resolved: "We cannot any longer defer the declaration of our determination to support with our lives and fortunes the supremacy of the British Constitution and the just dependence of the Canadas upon the British Crown."

All the regular troops in the province had been sent to Lower Canada while the militia anxiously waited to be called up. Macdonald was, of course, a member of the Sedentary Militia, as every able-bodied male in Upper Canada between the ages of 18 and 60 was required to serve. It was a vast, cumbrous and comically inefficient organization, which existed not so much to give the population adequate military training as to acquaint them with their responsibilities for the defence of the province and to muster them swiftly in times of danger. Once a year, on Training Day – June 4, King George III's birthday – they went through a few simple manoeuvres and then adjourned for sports, picnics and boisterous drinking. On the eve of the rebellions, British-born Anna Jamieson described a parade held at Erindale near Toronto:

"A few men, well-mounted, and dressed as lancers in uniforms which were, however, anything but uniform, flourished backwards on the green sward... themselves and their horses equally wild, disorderly, spirited, un-disciplined: but this was perfection compared to the infantry. Here there was no uniformity attempted of dress, of appearance, of movement; a few had coats, others jackets; a greater number had neither coats nor jackets, but appeared in their shirt sleeves, white or checked, clean or dirty, in edify-ing variety! Some wore hats, others caps, others their own shaggy heads of hair. Some had firelocks, some had old swords suspended in their belts or stuck in waistbands; but a greater number shouldered sticks or umbrellas... Now they ran after each other, elbowed and kicked each other, straddled, stooped and chattered; and if the commanding officer turned his back for a moment, very coolly sat down on the bank to rest... The parade day ended in a drunken bout and a riot, in which, as I was afterwards informed, the colonel had been knocked down... but it was taken so very lightly that I soon ceased to think about the matter."

On Wednesday morning, December 6, the regular stagecoach from the west, which had left Toronto on Sunday, arrived in Kingston. It bore the alarming news that rebels were about to attack the capital. That night, the magistrates called a meeting at the courthouse. As regular troops had left for Lower Canada, they informed the assembled citizens that they must improvise their own defence.

Their first duty was to defend Fort Henry and the naval base and to secure the eastern part of the province. Two Frontenac regiments mustered companies. A company of Lennox and Addington militia tramped into town, and other eager citizens not included in the existing militia formations joined independent companies and volunteered as artillerymen and civic guards. Detachments were dispatched to Fort Henry, Point Frederick, the Tête du Pont barracks, and to the blockhouses around the town. The Frontenac Dragoons careened about on horseback. Kingston was proud of its hastily collected amateur army of over 500 men, and the "loyal ladies" of the town, meeting at the Commercial Bank, quickly raised enough money to buy colours for their husbands and sons.

But there was little to do. There was drill and target-practice, some marching and counter-marching, but there was no fighting as Kingston and the surrounding area remained tranquilly loyal. The rebellion collapsed in a little skirmish on Yonge Street in Toronto.

Macdonald, the future prime minister of Canada, shouldered his musket with the rest. "I carried my musket in 1837," he wrote years later. "The day was hot, my feet were blistered – I was but a weary boy – and I thought I should have dropped under the weight of the flint musket which galled my shoulder. But I managed to keep up with my companion, a grim old soldier who seemed impervious to fatigue."

A few months later, Macdonald was defending rebels in a Kingston courtroom.

The Macdonald family homestead at Hay Bay, near Kingston. John A. Macdonald walked three miles to school each day. "Ye'll hear something of Johnny yet," his father said. (PAC)

🐚 THE REBELLION IN LOWER CANADA

A lawyer, seigneur and politician, Louis-Joseph Papineau's demands for reform spark an open rebellion in Lower Canada in 1837.

HE WAS AN UNLIKELY rebel. His father had carried dispatches through the American lines for Guy Carleton at the siege of Quebec, and he himself had served in the militia as a staff captain and was present at the capture of Detroit. A seigneur, handsome, intelligent, well-educated and rich, Louis-Joseph Papineau was quintessentially a member of the establishment. Speaker of the Assembly of Lower Canada for 22 years, he summed up his political beliefs on the occasion of the death of King George III in 1820:

"Since George III succeeded Louis XV of France, the reign of law has succeeded to that of violence; since that day the treasure, the fleet and the armies of Great Britain have been employed to provide us with an effective protection against all foreign danger; since that day her best laws have be-

RIGHT: *Louis-Joseph Papineau (1786-1871), leader of the Patriotes, was an unlikely rebel. First elected to the legislative assembly of Lower Canada in 1809, he emerged as the leader of a nationalistic party, the Parti Canadien (later the Parti Patriote). Made speaker in 1815, he began working for the reform of Lower Canada's political institutions. An address to a rally at St-Charles in 1837 led to open rebellion. Papineau fled to the U.S. and then to France, where he remained until pardoned in 1844. He then returned from exile in 1845.* (PAINTING BY THÉOPHILE HAMEL)

OPPOSITE PAGE: *Although Papineau espoused patience in October 1837, the crowd of 5000 demanded action.* (BIBLIOTHÈQUE NATIONALE DU QUEBEC)

come ours, while our faith, our property and the laws by which they were governed have been conserved; soon afterwards the privileges of her free constitution were granted us... All these advantages have become our birthright, and will be, I hope, the lasting heritage of our prosperity. In order to conserve them, we should act like British subjects and free men."

The shift in his opinions that eventually turned him into a revolutionary leader was gradual and reflected the fundamental French Canadian anxiety about their survival as a people. Concerned with large-scale immigration into Canada, which was upsetting the population balance, he increasingly became aware that the French had no real political power. Although they held a majority of seats in the Legislative Assembly, it was the English-speaking merchants of the Château Clique who had the governor's ear, monopolizing government appointments and brazenly exploiting their positions to enrich themselves. Every attempt by Papineau and his followers to make the government more responsive was dismissed as treachery. "It is not enough to send among us avaricious egotists to enrich themselves at the expense of Canadians, and then to enslave them," said Edouard Rodier, a member of the extremist group in the Assembly. "They must also rid themselves of their beggars and cast them by the thousands on our shores."

After three French Canadians were killed by British troops in an election riot in 1832, compromise became impossible. The Assembly passed the "Ninety-Two Resolutions," a catalogue of French Canadian grievances whereby imported goods were boycotted, and Patriotes, clad in homespun "Étoffe de pays" and carrying a rebel tricolour, took to the streets to do battle with the "Doric Club," a gang of young upper-class, English Cana-

An artillery battery fires at the front entrance of the church at St. Eustache. Illustration by C. Beauclerk. (NAC)

dian toughs. Street clashes degenerated into open revolt. On November 16, 1837, the government issued arrest warrants for 26 Patriote leaders, including Papineau, on charges of treason. Most escaped to the Richelieu Valley south of Montreal.

At St. Denis, on November 23, the Patriotes won their only victory, repulsing a hastily assembled militia force. Unfortunately, they murdered a prisoner, Lieutenant George Weir, as he tried to escape. A few days later, British troops drawn in from all the colonies fought their way into St. Charles. "On entering the town," a British officer recalled, "there was little quarter given, almost every man was put to death; in fact, they fought too long before thinking of flight. Many of them were burned alive in the barns and houses which were fired as they would not surrender." At least 150 Patriotes were killed. The few that escaped included a young law student, George-Étienne Cartier.

On December 14, the British commander, Sir John Colborne, a veteran of Waterloo, turned his attention to the village of St. Eustache, north of the island of Montreal. Led by Dr. Jean-Olivier Chénier, the Patriotes were forced out of their positions into the parish church. Retreating into the choir loft, they cut away the stairs and opened fire on British troops sheltered behind the altar. The church caught fire. "The position of the rebels in the church was critical and getting more dreadful by the moment," a witness said. "Soon the flames reached the point where they had to flee, but flight was difficult. Some of them just couldn't make it, and later they found their bodies, burned to a crisp. Dr. Chénier, seeing that all hope was lost, gathered some of his men together, and they jumped out the windows on the convent side. He wanted to try to break through the attackers and

Back view of the church at St. Eustache and the dispersal of the insurgents, December 14, 1837. Illustration by C. Beauclerk. (NAC)

escape, but he couldn't get out of the graveyard, and soon, struck by a shot, he fell and died almost immediately."

The surviving Patriotes tried to surrender, but someone in the British ranks shouted, "Remember George Weir" and they were shot down. Colborne was known ever after in Quebec as *Vieux Brûlot* (Old Firebrand).

The worst destruction was wrought by militia units that conducted a campaign of systematic terror. At St. Benoît, Joseph Girouard described "scenes of devastation and destruction more atrocious than any seen in a town taken by storm and given over to pillage after a long, hard siege. After completely pillaging the village, the enemy set fire to it and reduced it from one end to the other to a heap of ashes. Then they went in different directions, ravaging and burning on their way… carrying their fire as far as the village of Sainte-Scholastique." He recalls inhabitants rounded up in his courtyard, "which as you know, is very large; they were lined up, and two cannon placed in the gateway were aimed at them, while they were told they would be exterminated in a few minutes. There were no insults and outrages which were not heaped upon them, no threats which were not made, to frighten them into revealing the hiding places of those whom the British called their leaders. Not one of them would give the least hint."

Papineau, Cartier, Rodier, and other rebel leaders fled to the United States at the end of November, but it was several months before the last sparks of resistance were extinguished. It took 6000 British troops to crush the revolt. Hundreds of Patriotes had been killed. Twelve of those who were captured were publicly hanged, and 58 were subsequently deported to Australia. In absentia, Papineau was declared guilty of high treason and condemned to death.

❧ GEORGE-ÉTIENNE CARTIER

A politician and Father of Confederation, Cartier was largely responsible for gaining French-Canadian support for union.

PRIME MINISTER OF QUEBEC, corporation lawyer, railway promoter, defender of British parliamentary traditions and Father of Confederation, Sir George-Étienne Cartier was a very busy man indeed. "He is active – too active," Macdonald wrote warily after appointing him to his cabinet as provincial secretary in 1855. He seemed unaware as yet that, in Cartier, he had found his most effective French-Canadian ally, a man he would come to call "my second self."

A stolid, square-faced man imbued with joie de vivre, immense physical powers, and an explosive manner in debate, Cartier was the pre-eminent Quebec politician of his day. A solid conservative backed by the clergy and the English-speaking business elite, he would transform the province's legal, business and educational institutions. An early biographer called him a

RIGHT: *No one collected this reward for Papineau and, like other leaders of the rebellion, he regained respectability. Most of those punished were the rank-and-file. (PAC)*

OPPOSITE PAGE: *Sir George-Étienne Cartier (1814-1873) was the prime minister of the Province of Canada in 1857-58 and 1858-62 before becoming one of the Fathers of Confederation. He was largely responsible for gaining French-Canadian support for the union of the country. (PAC)*

4,000 Piastres de Recompense !

GOSFORD.

PROCLAMATION.

LOUIS JOSEPH PAPINEAU,

RECOMPENSE DE

MILLE LIVRES,

(Signe,) D. DALY.

"patriot, reformer, statesman and nation-builder," one of "the great founders" of Canada – quite a transformation for a rebel with a price on his head.

In 1837, the young law student had been among the Patriotes who met in the Hotel Nelson in Montreal to form the Sons of Liberty, a group modelled on the American revolutionary organization of the same name. Threatened with arrest after a street clash with a Tory "axe-handle brigade," he fled to St. Antoine in the Richelieu Valley, the very centre of revolutionary activity. On October 23, he participated in a six-county rally in St. Charles that demanded the popular election of magistrates and militia officers. His brother helped organize demonstrations in Verchères. Cartier spoke after mass in St. Antoine, but was unable to incite the village to rebellion, since, according to one hostile newspaper, "at the muster, his regiment, including himself, numbered only four people."

He fought at St. Denis, crossing the Richelieu under fire to return with ammunition and reinforcements. From boats at the river's edge, he and a hundred fresh, well-armed men stepped ashore to drive into the besieging militia's right flank, putting them to flight. After the retreat of government forces, he and his men spent nine days rallying resistance, felling trees across the main roads, and building rudimentary fortifications. Local support, however, dwindled quickly. The *curé* of St. Denis refused the sacraments to rebel supporters. With the approach of British troops, he and a companion fled to a swamp then separated to make their own way into exile.

Despite reports that he had frozen to death, Cartier spent the winter hidden with a cousin in a farmhouse near St. Antoine. Their stay ended when they became over-attentive to their host's maid. Noticing two pairs of legs sticking through a stovepipe hole in the ceiling, the maid's suitor – "as jealous as a Turk" – threatened to inform the authorities. Forced to flee, the Cartiers, hidden in barrels, crossed into the United States at Rouses Point. Cartier made his way to Plattsburgh, journeyed south to see Papineau in Saratoga, and finally settled in Burlington, Vermont. At home, he was charged with treason.

Following his acquittal, within a decade his life had changed dramatically. Married, a successful lawyer, a captain in the Montreal militia and a member of the Legislative Assembly, he was well launched on a triumphant career in Canadian politics.

Today, a bust of Cartier adorns the Quebec National Assembly, his statue faces Parliament in Ottawa, and Montreal honours his memory with parks, schools, and an 87-foot statue bearing the inscription: "Above All Be Canadian."

BELOW: *The battle of St. Denis. The Patriots repel an attack by regulars and volunteers, earning a short-lived victory. Cartier later fled to the U.S. (JOHN ROSS ROBERTSON COLLECTION)*

OPPOSITE PAGE: *The Battle at Montgomery's Tavern, with Samuel Peters Jarvis leading the Queen's Rangers.*

🐚 THE REBELLION
IN UPPER CANADA

*A Scottish-born Canadian journalist
and politician, William Lyon Mackenzie
rallies a rebel force at Montgomery's
Tavern in Toronto.*

IF PAPINEAU WAS AN unlikely revolutionary, William Lyon Mackenzie was a born rebel. A fiery bantam of a man, he was an unsparing, relentless critic of the established order in his adopted Upper Canada.

Born in Dundee, Scotland, he emigrated to Canada in 1820. Elected to the Assembly and ejected three times – first when York was incorporated into the City of Toronto – he was the publisher of the muckraking *Colonial Advocate*, and the sworn enemy of the Family Compact, the local version of the Château Clique. Imbued with radical and republican ideals and in close touch with Papineau's Patriotes, he was not opposed to the use of force to achieve his ends. In November 1837, when regular troops were sent to Lower Canada to deal with the anticipated revolt, he issued his own call to arms:

"Canadians! The struggle will be of short duration in Lower Canada, for

William Lyon Mackenzie (1795-1861) was elected in 1834 as the first mayor of Toronto. In December 1837, after numerous expulsions from and re-elections to the legislative assembly, he led an armed force down Yonge St. towards Toronto. The party was intercepted by the local militia and Mackenzie fled to the United States. He spent 13 years in exile until pardoned, then returning to Toronto in 1849 and again served as a member of the Ontario legislature. (ONTARIO ARCHIVES)

the people are united as one man… If we rise with one consent to over-throw despotism, we will make quick work of it… With governors from England we will have bribery at elections, villainy and perpetual discord… but independence would give us the means to enjoy many blessings."

When fighting broke out in Lower Canada, he decided to move on City Hall where enough weapons to equip thousands of men were guarded by just two constables. Early on the morning of December 7, mounted on a white horse, red wig askew and wrapped in layers of overcoats to protect himself against bullets, he assembled a most unmilitary mob of 300 men at Montgomery's Tavern and marched down Yonge Street. Marching up Yonge Street were the York militia, some 1500 strong, accompanied by local dig-nitaries and hundreds of unarmed civilians. "We saw the Lieutenant-Gov-ernor in his everyday suit," a witness recalled, "with one double-barrelled gun in his hand, another leaning against his breast, and a brace of pistols in his leathern belt. Also Chief Justice Robinson, Judges Macaulay, Jones, and McLean, the Attorney-General, and the Solicitor-General with their mus-kets, cartridge-boxes and bayonets, all standing in the ranks as private sol-diers under the command of Colonel Fitzgibbon." The Family Compact, it seemed, had come out to fight in person.

The two groups collided just south of what is now St. Clair Avenue. Joseph Gould, who was with the rebel force, described the scene: "We had no arms but our rifles, and some had only rude pikes and pitchforks. The troops, besides their muskets and plenty of ammunition, had two small

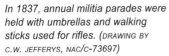

In 1837, annual militia parades were held with umbrellas and walking sticks used for rifles. (DRAWING BY C.W. JEFFERYS, NAC/C-73697)

field-pieces – one controlled by a friend of ours, and the other by an enemy. The friend fired grapeshot, and fired over us into the tops of the trees, cutting off the dead and dry limbs of the hemlocks, which, falling thickly amongst us, scared the boys as much as if cannonballs had been rattling around us. The other gun was fired low, and so careless that I did not like it. One of the balls struck a sandbank by my feet and filled my eyes with sand, nearly blinding me… Captain Wideman was killed on my left side… But we got to the west of the troops. They then turned and crossed to Yonge Street behind us."

The shooting lasted for 20 minutes and Wideman was the only man killed on either side. The rebels then broke and fled, while militiamen burned Montgomery's Tavern. Most of the volunteers who had flocked into the city from all over the province, lustily singing "Huzza for England, May she claim our fond devotion ever!" never heard a shot fired in anger.

Susannah Moodie, whose husband was with them, recalled: "In a week, Moodie returned. So many volunteers had poured into Toronto that the number of friends was likely to prove as disastrous as that of the enemies, on account of the want of supplies to maintain them all. The companies from the back townships were remanded and I received with delight my own again."

Despite a major manhunt, Mackenzie escaped across the border into the United States from where he directed small-scale and futile incursions over the next year. Reform in the Canadas would come about by peaceful means.

✍ WITH THE COBOURG RIFLES

In towns, villages, and settlements back of beyond, the militia rallied to march on Toronto.

"THE CITY HAS BEEN in an uproar all night," William Weller, stagecoach proprietor, wrote. Rumour ran riot. Sixty thousand rebels were said to be on the march and Indians were reported to have massacred the residents of Markham. After burning Montgomery's Tavern and routing Mackenzie and his men, Lieutenant-Governor Sir Francis Bond Head took counsel of his fears and dispatched couriers in all directions with orders to muster the militia to "raise the siege of Toronto" and "protect the unity of the Empire!"

Weller rode into Peterborough at midnight and, by daybreak, 1000 men were assembled outside the courthouse. In Douro Township, Samuel Strickland cleaned his double-barrelled shotgun and road off into a blinding snowstorm to bring the news to his neighbours, the John W. Dunbar Moodies and Thomas Traills. "My beloved husband goes at dawn," Mrs.

RIGHT: *Colonel Samuel Strickland (standing at right), with his family, brought news of the militia muster to his Peterborough neighbours.* (PAC/ c-45005)

OPPOSITE PAGE: *Although most of militiamen of the 19th century were equipped largely with their own sporting rifles, they were crucial to the defence of this country.* (MCCORD MUSEUM OF CANADIAN HISTORY)

Traill wrote, "and Moodie went with him, limping along on a broken leg." An old man, shouting that "the Yankees wounded me at New Orleans and I'll never die until I have a shot at them!" could not be kept from the march.

At Brockville, the Queen's Royal Borderers called for recruits. Each man was offered "eight dollars bounty, a new suit of clothes, and a great coat & pair of Boots, also a free Gift of 60 days pay when discharged." To which inducement was added an implied threat: "Let no Man pretending to LOYALTY HANG BACK!"

Moodie and Traill and the belligerent old man set off with 400 ill-equipped volunteers at 11 o'clock in the morning, under the command of Captain A. Cowall, formerly of the 1st Royals. They marched 17 miles the first day, stopping at every tavern along the way. At Port Hope, they were joined by the 2nd and 4th Battalions of the Northumberland Militia with two suspected spies in tow and 200 Indians from Rice Lake. They bedded down for the night in and around Graham's Tavern. It had been hoped that the steamer *Traveller* would transport them to Toronto on her regular run down the lake. Unfortunately, her captain passed them by, ignoring gunfire and frantic signals from the shore.

At Cobourg, the *Star* announced that "we are proud and gratified to say, that all the leading Reformers in the town have to a man denounced the present measures of Mackenzie, and are to a man actively aiding the arrangements to oppose him."

As gentlemen of the town rallied to the colours, a meeting was held at the Albion Hotel where a large sum was pledged to care for their families while they were away. "The men were all gone," Frances Stewart wrote, "and women and children had to attend to the stock and procure firewood, etc. The fear and uncertainty about the enemy kept those of us at home in a state of great anxiety." Adding to their anxiety, some officers, "drest in a little brief authority," refused their men permission to go home for a few hours under threat of imprisonment and confiscation of their property.

A company of 40 men, under the command of Captains D. Warren and E. McDonald, both of whom had served in the regulars, set out for Toronto a few days before the arrival of Bond Head's courier "amidst the cheers of the inhabitants." Three more companies and the "cavalry" left a day later.

They were in high spirits and marched on manfully, proud of their position as the advance guard of the volunteer army that was gathering in towns and villages, townships back of beyond, and along bush roads throughout the district. There were the Haldimand Volunteers, Moodie and Traill and their companions from Peterborough, the Northumberland Militia, the Cramahae Militia, and companies from Trent, Tweed and Colborne. Bond Head marvelled that "from the Newcastle District alone, 2600 men, with nothing but the clothes in which they stood, marched in the depth of winter towards the capital, although nearly 100 miles from their home." Throughout his domain, ten to twelve thousand men were on the march.

The day was fine and it was not unpleasant to march along dirt roads to the "nods, winks, and wreathed smiles of country girls." The Cobourg Rifles passed through Port Hope, enlivened by cheering crowds, and continued on to De la Rey's Tavern, which they reached a little after dark. Youngsters headed for the bar, while "the old and knowing" sought out bedrooms, "taking the precaution to put the keys in their pockets." Only 14 of 40 secured beds, the others had to make the most of the one that remained. It collapsed under the weight of eight rowdy Riflemen. After a battle in their bedclothes, it was decided that the mattress should be placed in the centre of the floor and that no one should lay more than his head on it.

Sleepless, they gathered round a bowl of punch to while away the night, while a storyteller told the tale of the Red Whale, a tale of the Sioux Indians. A youth of 17, in the last stages of consumption, read a poem entitled "The Time To Die," reflecting upon his condition. As he was reciting the last verse, a stranger entered the room and observed: "The time to die may be nearer than some of you young jokers imagine."

After a breakfast of pork and boiled potatoes, the Rifles shouldered arms and with three cheers for the Queen, resumed the march. Expecting an ambush at any moment, they anxiously scanned every clump of trees and turn of the road. It began to rain and the roads were churned into a muddy morass. Cold and wet, the consumptive youth set the tone as he rode along on a pony murmuring lines from Ossian: "Happy are they who die in their youth while their renown is around them!" Exhausted, they stumbled into Bowmanville to be quartered with the residents. A "True Briton" reported that "good order and quietness prevailed everywhere."

As they plodded along the next morning, the Rifles were joined by a young Irishman and his sisters who were travelling by cart to Toronto to seek work as servants. "Full of laughter and spirit," they cheered the men and offered them bread and cheese. A mouth organ sounded a note and they broke into *Old King Cole*, the regimental song. After a march of 18 miles, they bedded down for the night on the floor of Lee's Tavern in Whitby. The long march had begun to tell and they were asleep almost immediately.

At first light, the Rifles were joined by the Cavan Volunteers and the Port Hope Militia, armed as they were with bayonets, sticks, shotguns and muskets, with and without locks. At Highland Creek, they went into action for the first time. A private recalled:

"Immediately, the cavalry galloped forward to cut off the retreat while the Cobourg Rifles, with muskets at the trail, gallantly dashed forward to engage the enemy hand-to-hand. The door of a house was forced open and the place was captured without a struggle. The prisoners which fell to our section consisted of one old woman, one old fur cap and a bushel of apples. The last of our prisoners we devoured on the spot."

An hour later, with blistered and bloody feet, they were marching along King Street.

The citizens of Toronto were out in force to cheer the Cobourg Rifles as they crossed the bridge over the Don that Mackenzie had tried to burn a few days before. "Everything bore the appearance of a seized city," a trooper said. "Houses, barricades, civilians in arms, sentries in all directions and bustle everywhere. The pigs in the gutter were stalking about with set-up bristles, and the tom-cats with set-up backs; the dogs looked as if they had been crunching dead men's bones."

With a population of 12,000 now almost doubled with militiamen, Toronto was celebrated for "intemperance houses." Every second door seemed to feature the sign, "Pipes, Tobacco and Whiskey Sold Here," and where there was no sign, two pipes laid crosswise flanked by a plug of tobacco served the purpose.

Sir Francis Bond Head was on hand to greet them as they formed up in a hollow square at Government House. "He did not inspect us very minutely, which was very kind of him, considering the state of our wardrobe," Captain Warren recalled. "We gave him three hearty cheers, three more for the Queen, and three more for the British flag which waved proudly over our heads. We forgot in that moment all our weariness and fasting and raggedness!"

Three cheers more and the Cobourg Rifles were off to see the sights.

Years later, a wistful veteran would tell his son, "Oh! It was a perfect groggery!"

LEFT: *Catherine Parr Traill, née Strickland (1802-1899), was a pioneer writer and botanist. In 1832 she immigrated to Canada with her husband and settled near Peterborough, next door to her sister Susanna Moodie. There, she wrote her most famous book,* The Backwoods of Canada *(1838), a factual and detailed account of the reality of living in Upper Canada. (JEAN MURRAY COLE)*

OPPOSITE PAGE: *An American Patriot handbill. (BUFFALO HISTORICAL SOCIETY)*

🐚 THE HUNTERS

Determined to "liberate" Canada, the Hunters boasted lodges in every town and village along the border, from Maine to Michigan.

THE HUNTERS OFFERED something for everyone, from idealism to initiations, secret signs, passwords, badges, codes and colourful ranks. There were at least four degrees of Hunter: the Snowshoe, the Beaver, the Master Hunter and the Patriot Hunter. All ranks swore one of the most long-winded oaths on record:

"I swear to do my utmost to promote Republican institutions and ideas throughout the world, to cherish them, to defend them; and especially devote myself to the propagation, protection, and defence of these institutions in North America. I pledge my life, my property, and my sacred honour to the Association; I bind myself to its interests, and I promise, until death, that I will attack, combat, and help to destroy, by all means that my superior may think proper, every power and authority of Royal origin, upon this continent; and especially never to rest till all tyrants of Britain cease to have any dominion nor footing whatever in North America. I further solemnly swear to obey the orders delivered to me by my superior, and never to disclose any such order, except to a brother Hunter of the same degree. So help me God."

The origin of the name is obscure. It may have been a translation of the name used by the Patriotes of Lower Canada and their American allies who called their societies "Les frères chasseurs" and used Vermont as their headquarters. Both lodges were similar, with special signals and esoteric names for high-ranking officers. Or, it may have been derived from the name of a little-known veteran of Mackenzie's uprising who escaped to the United States after hiding for several days in an oven in a bakery several miles east of Toronto. Whatever its origins, the Hunters posed a far greater threat to Upper Canada than William Lyon Mackenzie and his ragtag band at Montgomery's Tavern.

As a triumphant Lieutenant Governor Sir Francis Bond Head marched up Yonge Street in December 1837, Mackenzie, red wig askew, hopped on a horse and headed for the border. Four days later, he reached Buffalo, N.Y., where he was welcomed as a hero and engulfed with offers of aid. Within a week, he had set up a republic on Navy Island, Canadian territory in the Niagara River, three miles above the falls. He created his own seal – a new moon breaking through the darkness – and designed a red, white, and blue republican flag replete with a galaxy of stars and stripes. Recruits, mostly Americans lured by promises of land grants, rallied to his cause.

Meanwhile, in Upper Canada, more than 10,000 militiamen were terrorizing those who had fought or sympathized with the rebels. Mackenzie's lieutenants, Sam Lount and Peter Matthews, were hung and close to 100 others deported. Property was plundered and burned and some 25,000 would leave the province in the months to come to escape reprisals. Along the Niagara frontier, drunken volunteers brawled in taverns and Orangemen baited Catholics. Neighbours turned against each other. At Chippewa, militiamen shook their fists and hurled insults across the river at Mackenzie and his men as they fortified Navy Island.

American recruits and supplies were brought to the island by the 26-ton paddle steamer *Caroline*. Shanties were built in the woods and Mackenzie barricaded his headquarters with fence rails before his followers opened fire on the troops drawn up along the shore. His wife arrived on December 29 and set to work making cartridge bags, "inspiring with her courage all with whom she conversed." That night, Captain Andrew Drew of the Royal Navy and 50 Canadian militiamen, armed with cutlasses, pikes, and pistols, stole aboard the *Caroline* at nearby Fort Schlosser. After a brief skirmish in which one American was killed, they set the ship afire and cut her loose. Blazing from stem to stern, she ran aground above the Horseshoe Falls and burned to the waterline.

Bombardment from Chippewa, quarrels with his subordinates, and pressure from the United States government drove Mackenzie from Navy Island in mid-January. Before him lay 11 difficult years. He was jailed for a year for breaking American neutrality laws then moved on to New York City where he eked out a meagre living as a clerk and journalist for the *New York Tribune*. He would not return to Canada until 1850.

As Mackenzie and his family slipped into poverty, the Hunters flourished. The first Hunter lodge was established in Vermont in the spring of 1838 and enjoyed widespread sympathy and support. New lodges bloomed in towns and cities from Maine to Michigan. Each new association brought additional recruits and the formation of more lodges, until the organization boasted a lodge in every town along the border.

Determined to liberate Canada, regardless of whether Canada wanted to be liberated or not, recruits from all walks of life flocked to the Hunters' standard. "Labourers left their employ; apprentices their masters; mechanics abandoned their shops; merchants their counters; husbands their families; children their parents; Christians their churches; ministers of the gospel their charges to attend meetings," a Master Hunter enthused.

The main lodges were situated at Rochester, Buffalo, Lockport, Cleveland, Detroit and Port Huron. Cleveland was home to the Grand Lodge of the west and Rochester its counterpart in the east, while Lockport headquartered the Canadian Refugee Relief Association. To avoid infiltration by government agents, an elaborate communications system was established between all lodges, officers of the order belonging to two or more of the associations, and employing their own secret signs and ciphers.

In September 1838, Cleveland hosted a weeklong convention of the

The arrival of Loyalist Volunteers at the Parliament Buildings, December 7, 1837. (DRAWING BY C.W. JEFFERYS, NATIONAL ARCHIVES OF CANADA)

leading Hunters. A.D. Smith, the city's justice of the peace, was elected president of the Republic of Canada. A grocer named Williams was elected vice-president and the posts of secretary-of-state, secretary-of-war and secretary-of-the-treasury were filled with other luminaries. Self-styled "Brigadier-General" Lucius Vergus Bierce, an Ohio lawyer, was appointed commander-in-chief of the republic-in-waiting's army, and clerks and shopkeepers were assigned to high command.

The Hunters also formed a navy. Gilman Appleby, late master of the *Caroline*, was named commander of the Patriot Navy in the west and Bill Johnson commodore of the eastern squadron. Johnson, the son of United Empire Loyalists, had become virulently anti-British. Convicted of smuggling, he had refused to serve in the militia in the War of 1812 and moved to Clayton, N.Y., where he spied for the Americans. From hideouts in the Thousand Islands that were all called Fort Wallace, he preyed on British shipping along the St. Lawrence, which earned him the title "Pirate Bill." Upgraded to admiral, he began to assemble a fleet.

To finance their fledgling armed forces, the Hunters organized the Republican Bank of Canada, offering 150,000 shares at $50 each. Tender was strictly gold and silver, although the bank hoped to eventually issue currency bearing the heads of murdered patriots and the legends "Death or Victory" and "Liberty, Equality and Fraternity." The sale of shares, alas, was less than brisk. Members came up with a paltry $300. Undaunted, the Hunters resolved that, upon the successful invasion of Canada, the bank would be funded with the proceeds of property seized from "traitors."

Disturbed by reports of the Hunters' activities, the governments of Upper and Lower Canada began to deploy troops along the border. Upper Canadians were enlisted in regular regiments. A detachment of militia was

RIGHT: *"If you're looking for truth, justice, or moral mercy you're wasting your time,"* the Caroline Almanack *said. It condemned the hanging of Samuel Lount and Peter Matthews.*

FAR RIGHT: *Peter Matthews (1786-1838) was a strong supporter of William Lyon Mackenzie. Captured after the rebels dispersed, he was hanged, together with Samuel Lount, on April 12, 1838, for treason.* (METROPOLITAN TORONTO LIBRARY)

kept at Whitby to deal with republican unrest in Reach and Pickering townships. Other detachments were dispatched to Baldwin and Dufferin Creeks, while gunboats sailed for Sarnia, Sandwich and Port Dover. Wherever regulars were required to march from their forts and posts, they were to be occupied by embodied militia. Sir John Colbourne, commander in both Canadas, was confident that a force of 1200 regulars could be conveyed to any trouble spot within two or three days.

Across the border, "General" John Ward Birge made plans for an invasion at Prescott and Fort Wellington, strategic positions on the lines of communication to Lower Canada. In January, Hunters aboard the schooner *Anne*, landed on Bois Blanc Island and shelled Fort Malden near Amherstburg before running aground. The crew, expecting to be greeted by thousands of eager freedom fighters, was taken into custody by irate locals. Hunters occupied Pelee Island for a few days and crossed the Niagara River. At Sarnia, they plundered homes and stores, while at Windsor they burned a barracks as a crowd cheered from Detroit rooftops. After delivering republican speeches, they were engaged by the militia. Before beating a hasty retreat, 25 were killed and 44 taken prisoner.

The bloodiest encounter was the November 12-16 Battle of the Windmill, near Prescott. More than 400 Hunters from Ogdensburg, New York, came ashore at Windmill Point and sheltered in a stone mill until they were routed by artillery and British regulars. Seventeen Americans and 16 British and Canadians troops lost their lives.

Disillusioned, the Hunters faded into obscurity. William Lyon Mackenzie, a man of whom it was said that no heaven on earth could please, was disillusioned too. Had he seen the American system sooner, he conceded, "I would have been the last man to rebel." In 1849, a Reform government allowed him to return to Canada. A year later, he came home to stay.

❧ BATTLE OF THE WINDMILL

At Prescott, Cornwall and along the St. Lawrence, the ringing of church bells announced the long-expected invasion of Canada.

NILS VON SCHOULTZ'S LIFE was a web of fact and fiction. Handsome, personable and bright, the 31-year-old émigré claimed to be a Polish exile who had fought the Russians. His father, a regimental commander, had been killed in action, he said, and his mother and sister exiled to Siberia.

In truth, he was Finnish-born and a Swedish national who briefly held a commission in the Polish Army. Taken prisoner by the Russians following the 1831 uprising, he escaped and joined the French Foreign Legion. A year later, he deserted and married an English girl in Florence. Unable to support her and two young children, he boarded ship to seek his fortune in the New World and, posing as a qualified chemist, found a job in a salt manufacturing plant in Salinas, New York. Passionate, idealistic and Catho-

RIGHT: *Of the prisoners taken at Prescott, Nils von Schoultz (pictured) and 11 others were hanged while the rest were transported to a penal colony on Van Diemen's Land (Tasmania).* (COURTESY ONTARIO ARCHIVES)

OPPOSITE PAGE: *At the Battle of the Windmill, November 12-16, 1838, American patriots attempted to "liberate" Canada from the British at Prescott, Ontario.* (FROM THE HISTORY OF LEEDS AND GRENVILLE)

lic, he soon joined the local anti-British Hunters Lodge, convinced that the people of Canada were as much oppressed as the Poles. In November 1838, true to his convictions, he took up arms and marched to Sackets Harbor with a hastily assembled force intent on liberating Canada.

"Major General" John Ward Birge, an Oswego lawyer, had been elected to lead the force. Unfortunately for the Hunters, he was singularly lacking in courage, intelligence, and military experience. Determined to take Prescott and Fort Wellington in a surprise attack and sever communications between Kingston and Montreal, he, like most Hunters, firmly believed that discontented Canadians would rally to the cause. He overlooked the inconvenient fact that the citizens of Prescott and the surrounding area were largely descendants of United Empire Loyalists and not enamoured with republican ideals.

An invasion of Canada had been expected throughout the summer and fall of 1838. Regulars and militia were deployed along the border and garrisons placed on full alert. At Fort Wellington, 100 Grenville militiamen and 35 Glengarries under the command of Colonel Plomer Young were ready to move out on a moment's notice. Sentries were posted at the wharves in Prescott and along the river. Even the press was aware that an invasion was imminent with the *Kingston Chronicle* reporting on November 7 that 500 men had passed through Watertown four days before, headed for Canada.

But Birge pressed on. On the morning of November 11, he and 200 men boarded two schooners at Oswego while 75 more went aboard the regular passenger steamer, the *SS United States* at Sackets Harbor. Keeping to themselves, they excited little interest among the crew or other passengers. At each of the steamer's regular stops, more and more men embarked. Ranging in age from 14 to 60, some were too drunk to stand.

As the *United States* rounded Cape Vincent, the captain was asked to take the approaching schooners in tow, a common practice of the day. Alongside, hatches were thrown open and scores of armed men in a bewildering array of homemade uniforms clambered aboard. There were epaulets and brass buttons, swords, and sashes. "Admiral" Bill Johnson, more commonly known along the St. Lawrence as "Pirate Bill," sported a red officer's sash adorned with five pistols of various calibres and a foot-long Bowie knife.

Near Morriston, the schooners were cut loose and promptly ran aground on a muddy delta at the mouth of the Oswegatchie River. Struggling ashore, the Hunters assembled at Windmill Point close to the little hamlet of New Jerusalem.

The ringing of church bells raised the alarm and the militia assembled to reinforce Fort Wellington. The Queen's Royal Borderers marched out of Brockville alongside the Leeds militia, and the 83rd Regiment at Kingston was alerted. The gunboat *Experiment* took up position in the river. When the commandeered *United States* returned to land reinforcements and supplies, she opened fire with her 18-pounder carronade, beheading the helmsman. General Birge, who was standing next to him, suddenly became "very ill" and ordered the steamer back to Ogdensburg. He was not seen again until the invasion was over.

Ashore, Nils von Schoultz took charge and marched 192 stranded Hunters into a nearby windmill and outbuildings on a bluff about the river. Six stories high, pierced with windows from top to bottom and built of solid stone, the windmill was a natural fortress. In a light rain, the Hunters took up position and unfurled their flag – an eagle and two stars on a blue background lovingly stitched by the ladies of Onondaga County. They settled down for the night convinced that they would be joined in the morning by hordes of downtrodden Canadians.

To their dismay, the Hunters awoke to find themselves surrounded by an ever-thickening circle of troops and gunboats on the river. After a miserable night marching in the rain, Royal Marines and some 500 men from Colonel Young's Glengarry, Grenville and Stormont and Dundas militias had taken up positions around the windmill and the buildings of New Jerusalem. At dawn, with the Marines in the vanguard, they formed up into two columns and attacked.

Von Schoultz quickly deployed his men in open order in the fields beyond the buildings. As the columns approached, they opened fire, killing 15 and wounding 60, the Canadian militia being the hardest hit. But they continued the attack, flanking the Hunters and forcing them back into the mill. Shot from the *Queen Victoria* and *Cobourg*, bounced off the walls without so much as damaging the mortar. As the day wore on, Young reluctantly came to the conclusion that it was pointless to proceed without heavy artillery and ordered a retreat. With darkness, the Hunters gathered the dead and treated the wounded on both sides as best they could with their meagre supplies.

Throughout the day, thousands had lined the American shore to cheer von Schoultz. But no help was forthcoming. Martial law was declared and regular troops occupied Ogdensburg, arresting prominent Hunters. General Birge was routed out of his sickbed, while Bill Johnson was picked up in the woods near Sackets Harbor. Cold, hungry and very much alone, von Schoultz and his men huddled in the mill as it began to snow.

Desultory fire continued the next day as Canadians and Americans tried to negotiate an end to the affair. An American proposal that the Hunters be permitted to surrender to the U.S. government and stand trial in New York State was turned down flatly by Colonel Young. The Hunters, he argued, had no hope of escaping as they had violated British neutrality and had killed and wounded 75 soldiers and militia. He insisted that they face a British court. When von Schoultz asked for terms, he was told there were none.

Late that afternoon, the artillery arrived along with four more companies of the 83rd. Two 18-pounders were placed on the gunboats and a howitzer was positioned on a knoll overlooking Windmill Point. Under the command of Major McBean of the Royal Artillery, they opened fire with devastating effect, reducing the buildings around the mill to piles of rubble. The Hunters, supplies and ammunition running low, returned the fire sporadically with a single cannon loaded with hinges, bolts and the odd six-pound ball picked up from British field pieces. As darkness fell, with 13 dead and 22 wounded, they ran up a white flag.

Broken in spirit and with their wounded untended, the survivors filed out of the windmill past lines of infuriated militiamen. Von Schoultz was captured by the river as he tried to escape. Paraded through Prescott, he and more than 100 Hunters were then herded aboard the *Cobourg* for transport to Kingston.

Roped together by their necks with von Schoultz in the lead, the Hunters were marched through the streets of Kingston to Fort Henry as crowds gathered to shout abuse and a band played "Yankee Doodle." Despite the able services of a promising young lawyer named John A. Macdonald, von Schoultz and 11 others were condemned to death by hanging. The first to be hanged, Nils von Schoultz died like a soldier, bravely and with dignity.

LEFT: *More than 100 Hunters were captured at the Battle of the Windmill, then paraded through the streets of Prescott and Kingston in chains. (toronto central library)*

OPPOSITE PAGE: *A total of 19 men were sent to the gallows for their part in the skirmishes near Montgomery's Tavern on 7 December 1837.*

MACDONALD FOR THE DEFENCE

The Rebellion made Macdonald's reputation as a lawyer, but the ghost of Nils von Schoultz would haunt him for the rest of his life.

IN THE BUSY JUDICIAL summer of 1838, the jails were crowded with rebels awaiting trial. John Montgomery languished at Fort Henry for no greater crime than owning a tavern in Toronto. In the Kingston jail, eight men from Hastings, Lennox and Addington counties were arraigned for bearing arms, coerced to sign affidavits admitting their guilt. Called to their defence, Macdonald won acquittals, a local newspaper informing its readers that "the prisoners were defended with much ingenuity and ability by Mr. J.A. Macdonald, who though one of the youngest barristers in the Province, is rapidly rising in his profession."

The case of Nils von Schoultz haunted Macdonald for the rest of his life. He may well have been in the crowd that gathered to watch as von Schoultz, his hands bound, strode proudly through the streets of Kingston at the head of a long sullen line of prisoners taken at the Battle of the Windmill. A tall, handsome and soft-spoken man with impeccable manners, he bore himself with stoical dignity. A Pole by birth, son of a cultivated and aristocratic family of Swedish ancestry, he had fought in the Polish uprising of 1830, studied in Paris, taught music in Florence and served in the Foreign Legion before emigrating to the United States.

At Salina, in northern New York State, he worked as a chemist. Here, under the influence of the Hunters, a violently anti-British organization, he reached the romantic conclusion that Canadians were as oppressed as the Poles. Determined to liberate them he came ashore at Windmill Point near Prescott and found himself the virtual leader of an abandoned army. Now, in the final days of November 1838, he faced a court martial at Fort Henry.

His co-defendants were terrified men, a newspaper reported, but von Schoultz was, "as unmoved as a rock." In a quiet voice he told the court that he had been terribly deceived and that the whole enterprise had been conceived and carried out in ignorance. He took full responsibility for his actions and pleaded guilty. Macdonald begged him to throw himself on the mercy of the court but he refused to change his plea and was sentenced to death. He was hanged on December 8.

Macdonald spent many hours with him before his death as he told the long, tangled story of his life. He drew up his will and a grateful von Schoultz tried to leave him a small legacy, which Macdonald was obliged to refuse. To the end of his days he remembered his story with unfaded clarity.

The Rebellion had made Macdonald's reputation as a lawyer. It had marked him, though. For him, and the people of Kingston, the "rebellion" had been not so much a local uprising as a series of American raids. From then on, he never lost a lingering anxiety for the problem of Canadian defence.

OPPOSITE PAGE: *John George Lambton, Earl of Durham (1792-1840), became the governor general and commissioner of British North America in 1838. As Lord Privy Seal in the administration of Lord Grey, he helped draft the Reform Bill of 1832. His detailed and famous 1839 report recommended a modified form of responsible government and a legislative union of the Canadas and the Maritime provinces.*

 RADICAL JACK

Sent to Lower Canada to investigate the Rebellion of 1837, Lord Durham recommended the union of the Canadas: "Two nations warring in the bosom of a single state."

DETERMINED TO END THE crisis in the colonies, the British government dispatched a new governor general to the Canadas in May 1838, to conduct a far-reaching inquiry into the rebellions. John George Lambton, first Earl of Durham, was a 33-year-old wealthy aristocrat who had briefly held an army commission. Affiliated with the liberal wing of the Whig party, his adversaries had nicknamed him "Radical Jack" for the significant role he had played in drafting the Great Reform Bill of 1832. Durham was granted extraordinary powers and an enormous budget.

"I beg you to consider me as a friend and arbitrator," he wrote in a proclamation to the people of Upper and Lower Canada, "ready at all times to listen to your wishes, complaints, and grievances, and fully determined to act with the strictest impartiality." His first step was to grant an amnesty to many of the Patriotes in the hope of restoring calm. One hundred and fifty were released on the day of Queen Victoria's coronation, while several others were exiled. Papineau and the other Patriote leaders who had found refuge in the United States faced the death penalty if they returned to Lower Canada. "Not one drop of blood has been shed," Durham wrote to the Queen. "The guilty have received justice, the misguided mercy, but at the same time, security is afforded to the loyal and peaceable subjects of this hitherto distracted province."

While Durham was preparing his report, another group of Patriotes, the Société des frères chasseurs, affiliated with the Hunters' Lodges in the United States, were about to launch an invasion, timed to coincide with an uprising in Lower Canada. In the autumn of 1838, three hundred frères chasseurs attacked the seigneurial manor of Beauharnois, taking 60 prisoners, including Edward Ellice, Durham's personal secretary. Ellice's wife Jane described his captors as terrifying revolutionaries, "the most ruffian looking men I ever saw except in my dreams of Robespierre." After six days in captivity, Ellice and the other prisoners were released. The rebels then hurried back across the border.

In the days ahead, the Glengarry Highlanders and other militia units, brought in from Upper Canada, burned and looted their way across the Beauharnois region. Janice Ellice witnessed the devastation: "The Glengarries' boast is 'No fear of our being forgotten, for we've left a trail six miles broad all thro' the country,'" she wrote. "They seem to be a wild set of men. One of them told me that the houses they had spared in coming down the country, they would surely burn in going back."

In the wake of the rebellions in the Canada, hundreds of imprisoned rebels had been convicted of high treason. Seventeen men had been hanged in Upper Canada, 12 in Lower Canada, and 130 prisoners were exiled to the penal colony of Australia. Ill-disciplined militia units like the Glengarries, delighted to be embodied and paid after a year of bad harvests and an economic depression, roamed the countryside. The constitution was suspended and the assemblies dissolved. The Family Compact and an English-speaking elite in Lower Canada reigned supreme. Government in the Canadas, according to Lord Durham, was in the hands of a "petty, corrupt, insolent Tory clique."

Durham set out to change all that, arguing in his *Report on the Affairs of British North America* that "it is not by weakening, but strengthening the influence of the people on its Government that I believe that harmony is to be restored." Durham's solution was responsible government, a system in which the executive would be drawn from the majority in the assembly. But his tenure in the Canadas was brief. He was recalled in October 1838 when the British government refused to sanction an illegal ordinance exiling a handful of political prisoners to Bermuda. "I little expected the reward I have received from home – disavowal and condemnation," he wrote. "In these circumstances I have no business here – My authority is gone – all that rests is military power, that can be better wielded by a soldier, and Sir John Colborne will, no doubt, do it efficiently."

In his famous report, Durham stated that there was a much more serious problem than governance in Lower Canada. "I expected to find a contest between a government and a people," he wrote. "I found two nations warring in the bosom of a single state: I found a struggle, not of principles, but of races; and I perceived that it would be idle to attempt any amelioration of the laws or institutions until we could first succeed in terminating the deadly animosity that now separates the inhabitants of Lower Canada into the hostile divisions of French and English."

Durham proposed to unite the two Canadas, firmly believing that the French, whom he described as a people "without history and without literature," living in "an old and stationary society in a new and progressive world," would ultimately benefit. "The language, the laws, the character of the North American Continent are English," Durham stated, "and every race but English appears there in a condition of inferiority. It is to elevate them from that inferiority that I desire to give the Canadians our English character."

The British government readily approved the union of the Canadas. It would not, however, grant responsible government – a term for which Durham denied paternity – fearing that colonial autonomy would lead to the breakup of the empire. Responsible government would not come until 1847 – ushered in by Durham's son-in-law, Lord Elgin.

₰ THE STRONG ARM OF ENGLAND

With England at war in India and the Crimea in the 1850s, British North Americans did their bit to defend their motherland.

IN THE YEARS BEFORE Confederation, British North America was facing pressure from both Britain and the United States. There were a number of war scares between Britain and the U.S., most of them not serious, and none of them initiated by the Canadas. As the closest British possession to the United States but with no power to control its own foreign affairs, Canada was always at risk, particularly in an age of remorseless American expansionism. As Thomas D'Arcy McGee, a future Father of Confederation, put it: "They (the United States) coveted Florida, and seized it; they coveted Texas and stole it; and then they picked a quarrel with Mexico, which ended by their getting California... had we not the strong arm of England over us, we would not have had a separate existence." But the "strong arm of England" was tiring.

RIGHT: *Dragoons and an 18-pounder gun crew in full dress uniform at Tête du Pont Barracks (Fort Frontenac in Kingston).*

OPPOSITE PAGE: *The first Canadian to receive the Victoria Cross was Lieutenant Alexander Dunn when he saved the life of a sergeant at Balaclava on September 15, 1833 during the Charge of the Light Brigade.* (IMPERIAL WAR MUSEUM)

Taxpayers, reasonably enough, resented the expense they had to bear to defend British North America. Moreover, the United States, bigger, more populous, and more prosperous, was becoming vastly more important to Britain than Canada. And British North America was not easily defended. It was sparsely populated and geographically and politically diverse. Newfoundland sat in splendid isolation; the separate colonies of Nova Scotia, New Brunswick, and Prince Edward Island had little to do with each other; and Upper and Lower Canada, merged into the United Province of Canada in 1840 following Lord Durham's report, was mired in political deadlock. Much of the northwest territory was still loosely held by the Hudson's Bay Company, and British Columbia, in the throes of a gold rush in the Cariboo country, was overrun with American prospectors.

Now that British North America had achieved responsible government, Lord Grey, the Secretary of State for War and the Colonies, argued that "they ought also pay all its expenses, including military protection." The governor general, Lord Elgin, disagreed. "Canada has a special claim for protection beyond any other colony because it is the fact of her connexion with Great Britain which exposes her to hostile aggression," he wrote. "She has no enemy to dread but the States, and they would cease to be dangerous to her if she were annexed… What you really want then is a sufficient body of troops to occupy the forts, to form a nucleus around which a great force composed of militia may be gathered in case of regular warfare, and to give the peaceful residents of the frontier who have the misfortune to dwell in the vicinity of a population combining the material force of high civilization with the loose political morality & organization of barbarous hordes, a reasonable security against marauding incursions."

Nevertheless, Lord Elgin eagerly sought to improve trade and relations with "the barbarous hordes." He achieved both in 1854, when British North America and the United States signed the Reciprocal Trade Agreement.

Throughout the 1840s, the British had maintained more than 10,000 regular troops in British North America and 21,000 provincial militia remained on continuous service. But as relations with the United States improved, the garrison began to shrink. The provincial troops were disbanded, gunboats paid off, and Kingston was closed as a naval base. The remaining troops were concentrated at Quebec and Halifax. The outbreak of the Crimean War completed the process, as virtually all the remaining troops were recalled to fight the czar. By 1855, fewer than 2000 regulars were left in the Canadas, but British taxpayers were still paying a hefty sum – £280,000 a year – for their upkeep. The war, however, unleashed a tide of enthusiasm for all things military, and for a time it appeared that Britain might well be able to shed its entire British North American defence burden.

Nova Scotia and New Brunswick expressed their imperial devotion in stirring resolutions and the formation of 30 volunteer companies, all willingly spending considerable sums of their own money to clothe and equip themselves. In the Canadas, the government hired British pensioners to guard abandoned forts – Fort Lennox was now a boys' reformatory, and Fort Malden a lunatic asylum – and announced plans to reform its militia system. The new post of adjutant general went to a half-pay British colonel, and new volunteer regiments of artillery, riflemen, and cavalry were formed. In his report, the adjutant general was optimistic: "The persons who have joined this Force are not the dissolute and the idle, but they are, on the contrary, the respectable Mechanics of the several Towns and Villages where the Companies of this Force are located." The volunteers of this Active Militia elected their own officers and paid for their own uniforms. For a time, many of them trained far more days than the number authorized and paid for by the government.

On Vancouver Island, Governor James Douglas promised to lead the Indians against Russian trading posts on the Pacific coast, if only the order came. In the meantime, he mustered the Victoria Voltigeurs, a motley collection of Hudson Bay Company employees, Métis and Indians, resplendent in tasseled caps and overcoats, white shirts with red sashes, buckskin trousers and moccasins. No Voltigeur was ever mistaken for a British regular. The Voltigeurs remained in service until the arrival of the Royal Engineers in 1858. The Engineers built roads, including the Cariboo Road from Yale to Bakerville on the mainland, laid out New Westminster, and discouraged American prospectors who regarded the annexation of British Columbia as part of their manifest destiny.

By the end of the decade, there were more than 18,000 militiamen happily parading in their spare time in towns and villages all across British North America. Officers were business or professional men, while other ranks were clerks, farmers, or artisans. Many of the most famous Canadian regiments were formed at this time, among them, the Queens Own Rifles, Royal Rifles of Canada, Canadian Grenadier Guards, Voltigeurs de Québec, Royal Hamilton Light Infantry, Hastings and Prince Edward Regiment, Governor General's Horse Guards, and the Royal Regiment of Canada.

Militia regiments had been raised in Canada before, but all were fencibles and committed to service in North America only. However, with the outbreak of the Crimean War followed by the Indian Mutiny a year later, Canadian volunteers were anxious to raise a regiment for imperial service. The unit would be added to the British Army list, bearing the name 100th (Prince of Wales' Royal Canadian) Regiment.

The regiment was raised in Upper Canada and consisted of twelve 100-man companies. The adjutant general of Canadian militia relinquished his post to become the regiment's first commanding officer. Alexander Dunn, who had won the Victoria Cross while serving with the 11th Hussars at Balaclava, became the senior major. Recruiting began in April 1858. Pay was at British army levels and an enlistment bounty of three guineas was awarded.

The new regiment sailed for England that summer, outfitted with uniforms which had been left over from the War of 1812. Many of these had

The Victoria Voltigeurs disbanded after two years, but regiments such as the Victoria Volunteer Rifles carried on the tradition. (MCCORD MUSEUM OF CANADIAN HISTORY)

rotted away. The regimental history records that in some cases the tails of the old swallowtail greatcoats had simply disintegrated. Packs were coated with tar that stained what was left of their tattered red tunics.

Man for man, the Canadians were probably better soldiers than the British. They were bigger, fitter, and most of them were literate. However, their independent spirit led to inevitable run-ins with the guards, sergeants, and aristocratic officers assigned to train them. A British orderly officer met his match when after asking if there were any complaints, a burly Canadian scathingly denounced the quality of his rations. When he told the angry soldier that he could do nothing about it, the Canadian replied: "Why the hell did you ask, then?" The guardrooms were frequently overflowing.

The Royal Canadians sailed for Gibraltar just as the Indian Mutiny was ending. Before leaving, they received colours from His Royal Highness the Prince of Wales and the motto "Pro Patria," which was later adopted by the much more famous Royal Canadian Regiment. From Gibraltar, the regiment moved on to Malta where Major Dunn took over command. The regiment served in India for a number of years before it was twinned with the 109th Bombay Infantry. By that time, most of the volunteers had returned home and the regiment's Canadian connections were all but forgotten. So, too, was Alexander Dunn, VC. He was killed in a mysterious hunting accident in Abyssinia in 1868 and is buried at Senafe, Ethiopia.

Enthusiasm for things military even extended to British North America's political class. George-Étienne Cartier, who had fought with the Patriotes in 1837 – "that damnable little French Canadian" according to *Globe* founder George Brown – wore a miniature of Napoleon around his neck and was

Lieutenant Alexander Dunn of the 11th Hussars, the first
Canadian awarded the Victoria Cross, earned the honour for his
actions at the Charge of the Light Brigade on October 25, 1854.
(NATIONAL ARCHIVES OF CANADA)

given to singing voyageur songs in public. "Mr. Cartier dined in full uniform! No one knows why," reported Frances Monck, the wife of the governor general, after a dinner party in Montreal in 1861. "Mr. Cartier sang, or
croaked after dinner and made everyone he could find stand up, hold hands
and sing a chorus." John A. Macdonald, who, as a young man, had marched
with the militia to put down the rebellion in Upper Canada, sometimes
wore a British ceremonial uniform to meet with visiting royalty. "A great
deal of time has been wasted by John A. Macdonald in learning to walk, for
the sword suspended from his waist has an awkward knack of getting between his legs, especially after dinner," Brown sniffed after one such meeting. Macdonald replied that the voters "would rather have a drunken John
A. Macdonald than a sober George Brown." The voters eventually got
both.

Canadians soon had enough of things military and, preoccupied with a
sharp economic downturn, turned their attention to more immediate concerns. The militia companies faded away. In 1861, a new adjutant general
of Canadian militia complained to the War Office that "the militia exists
alone on paper, and although nominally officered, they are generally speaking too old for service (in some cases from 60 to 90 years of age), entirely
unacquainted with their Duty, totally ignorant of Drill, and without Adju-
tants and Staff." Worse still, he reported that the legislature "has repeatedly
refused to provide money for the purpose of Defence."

That was about to change. On April 12, 1861, at Fort Sumter in South
Carolina, the first shots were fired in the American Civil War, a war that
threatened to engulf Canada.

❧ THE AMERICAN CIVIL WAR

Although it was an American tragedy, the Civil War was a defining moment in Canada's history. Fear of invasion and the political fallout of the war were the catalysts to Confederation.

THERE HAS BEEN NOTHING like it on American soil before or since. A devastating confrontation that threatened to tear the United States apart, the Civil War pitted brother against brother, family against family, and state against state. The names of its great battles resonate still: Antietam, Chickamauga, the Five Forks, Gettysburg, Shiloh, Vicksburg, and the Wilderness. So, too, do the names of the generals: Grant and Lee, Sherman and Longstreet, Sheridan, Forrest, Jeb Stuart, and Stonewall Jackson. Above all, the name of Abraham Lincoln lives on, the tragic president who became a victim of the war. Before it came to an end at a courthouse at Appomattox in 1865, more than a million of America's young men had been killed or wounded, entire cities and once-productive farm-

RIGHT: *Southerners responded to the call for recruits. Here, newly recruited men of the 9th Mississippi Infantry gather round a campfire.* (LIBRARY OF CONGRESS)

OPPOSITE PAGE: *Of the 50,000 Canadians who served on both sides of the conflict in the American Civil War, some 5000 died in battle.* (JOHN L MCGUIRE COLLECTION)

lands lay in ruins, and a way of life had vanished forever.

Although it was an American tragedy, the Civil War was a defining moment in Canada's history. Tens of thousands of Canadians fought in the war, caught up in what they saw as the romance and excitement of it all, or attracted by generous signing bonuses offered by Northern recruiters. At least 5000 died, and thousands more returned home wounded in body and spirit. The war also marked the initial influx of draft dodgers – "skedaddlers" as they were called then. Of the 776,000 men drafted into the Union army, 161,000 "failed to report," many of them fleeing to Canada. They joined the approximately 30,000 escaped slaves who had come by the Underground Railroad to a Canada they saw as Canaan, the Promised Land.

When the war began in 1860, most Canadians were overtly sympathetic to the North. Slavery in the South was seen as an abomination and geographical proximity to the border states inevitably led to trade and close personal and family ties, as Canadians and Americans traveled freely back and forth across the border. As the war went on, however, Canadian sympathies underwent a dramatic transformation, as relations between Britain and the United States deteriorated and Canada was threatened with invasion. In the Maritimes, where blockade running continued to supply the South with munitions and material, Southern sympathies were soon running so high that many businesses openly flew Confederate flags and traded in Confederate currency. Conservative newspapers in the Canadas became increasingly critical of the North and many were openly pro-Southern. In the last year of the war, as the tide turned against the South, Southern leaders found Canada a convenient base of operations. Spies and saboteurs crossed the border to raid and loot. One group attempted to firebomb hotels and public buildings in New York City, while another sacked the town of St. Albans, Vermont. None of these forays were particularly successful, but they angered the North and fueled a movement to annex Canada. Fear of invasion, and the economic and political fallout of the war, were the catalysts to Confederation.

Britain's attitude towards the war was summed up in a ditty published in *Punch*:

> *Though with the North we sympathize*
> *It must not be forgotten*
> *That with the South we've stronger ties*
> *Which are composed of cotton.*

Although Britain was officially neutral, the mercantile and upper classes – like those in Canada – echoed Lord Palmerston's complaint that the Americans were "the most disagreeable fellows to have to do with." Lincoln's election in 1860 spurred hopes that this entirely unpleasant country might disappear, leaving behind the "gentlemanly" and cotton-rich Southern planters. The middle class, as deeply moved by Harriet Beecher Stowe's immensely popular anti-slavery polemic *Uncle Tom's Cabin* as most Canadians were, tended to favour the North. Canadians, however, could express their preference in a very tangible way – by enlisting in the Union armies, which more than 40,000 eventually did.

Britain's unofficial attitude towards the United States was reflected in its foreign policy which almost led to war in 1861. On November 8, less than a year after the Confederates opened fire on Fort Sumter, an American warship, the *San Jacinto*, stopped the British mail packet *Trent* in the Gulf of Mexico and arrested two Confederate agents on their way to Europe on a diplomatic mission. They were imprisoned in Boston, and the British, outraged at this supposed breach of international law, demanded redress. "I don't know whether you are going to stand for this," Palmerston thundered at a cabinet meeting, "but I'll be damned if I do!" Palmerston demanded an apology and the release of the Confederate agents. In the meantime, he dispatched 14,000 troops to Canada. Lord Newcastle, the colonial secretary, wrote to Governor General Charles Stanley Monck: "You must have heard of the affair of the *Trent* and the serious implications which it must produce. I am bound to warn you that war is too likely to be the result… Every preparation should be made to defend Canada from invasion."

Some Americans welcomed the prospects of war. "In the event of England in her folly, declaring war on against the United States," the *New York Herald* proclaimed, "the annexation of the British North American possessions will unavoidably follow. We could pour 150,000 troops into Canada in a week, and overrun the province in three weeks more. In this invasion, we should be aided by a large portion of the inhabitants, two-thirds of whom are in favour of annexation with the United States."

This was indeed news to most Canadians. "I do not believe it is our destiny to be engulfed into a Republican Union," Thomas D'Arcy McGee wrote. "We can hardly join the Americans on our own terms and we never ought to join them on theirs. A Canadian nationality, not French-Canadian, nor British-Columbian, nor Irish-Canadian – patriotism rejects the prefix – is, in my opinion, what we should look forward to – and that is what we ought to labour for, that is what we ought to be prepared to defend to the death."

Fortunately, cooler heads prevailed. In Washington, U.S. Secretary of War William Seward grudgingly apologized for the "Trent" affair and the Confederate commissioners were released. Seward even went as far as inviting the troops Palmerston had dispatched to land at Portland, Maine, from which they could take the British-owned Grand Trunk Railway to Canada. Palmerston would have none of it, however, and insisted on marching them up the Tamicousta Road, the winter trail through New Brunswick which ran from Fredericton to Quebec City.

Unfortunately, as the threat of invasion receded, garrison towns in Canada themselves became battlegrounds for bored soldiers and resentful locals. In towns throughout Upper Canada, public buildings were taken over for barracks and rents doubled. In Halifax, an argument over who had won a greasy-pole climbing contest at a fall fair erupted into a gang fight between soldiers and civilians. Drunkenness and prostitution were widespread. So, too, was desertion, as disgruntled soldiers found their way across the border to enlist in the Union armies.

A militia bill was introduced in the Canadian legislature in 1862, prodded by Governor General Monck and supported by the Macdonald-Cartier coalition. A parliamentary commission reported that the Canadas needed an active militia of 50,000 and a reserve force of a similar size. The active force, consisting of the existing volunteers as well as men selected by ballot from the Sedentary Militia, was to drill for fourteen to twenty-eight days a year. Committees met to formulate plans for fortifications and one hundred thousand rifles were ordered from Britain. However, Macdonald knew that there was little support for the bill and repeatedly delayed it. He finally introduced the bill with a disjointed speech, then disappeared. "Mr. J.A. Macdonald," Monck observed dryly, "was prevented from attending his place in the House during the whole of last week, nominally by illness but really as everyone knows, by drunkenness."

The bill was defeated after 15 French-speaking members from Lower Canada defected and Macdonald's government resigned. A.A. Dorien, the leader of the opposition Rouges, argued that French-Canadian boys would be torn from their farms to fight in Britain's wars, while George Brown saw no reason that "Canada should provide entirely for her defence when she is not the author of the quarrels against the consequences of which she is called to stand upon her guard." There were many reasons for the defeat of the defence bill, but not for the first time or the last Canadians had refused to accept responsibility for their own defence.

There was outrage in London. "Canada," *The Times* said, "has learned to trust others for the performance of services for which weaker and less wealthy populations are wont to rely exclusively on themselves." *The Spectator* was more succinct. "It is, perhaps, our duty to defend the Empire at all hazards," an editorial read, "it is no part of it to defend men who will not defend themselves."

A succession of Confederate-inspired incidents along the border, culminating in the St. Albans raid in 1864 and the foolish release of the raiders by a Canadian court heightened tensions. A Union general ordered "all military commanders to cross the boundary into Canada and pursue the rebels wherever they take refuge." President Lincoln revoked the order, but immediately terminated the Reciprocity Treaty and threatened to place gunboats on the Great Lakes and Lake Champlain in violation of the Rush-Bagot Agreement of 1817. For the first time, Canadians were required to produce passports to enter the United States.

Tension along the border hurried Canadian politicians to Charlottetown to promote the idea of Confederation. A host of reasons backed the idea: political deadlock in the Canadas, the dream of western expansion, gaining credits to build railways, even personal ambitions. But every problem was linked to the fear of war and invasion. To protect itself, British North America would have to be united.

"War or no war, the necessity of placing these provinces in a thorough state of defence can no longer be postponed," George Brown said as he boarded the *Queen Victoria* for the journey to Charlottetown. "And we can do this efficiently and economically by the union now proposed."

Macdonald, Cartier, Alexander Galt, and D'Arcy McGee were also aboard the *Queen Victoria*, a 190-tonne steamer. "We had great fun coming down the St. Lawrence," Brown wrote, "having fine weather, a broad awning to recline under, excellent stores of all kinds, an exceptionable cook, lots of books, chessboards, backgammon and so forth." They occupied themselves by discussing the proposed union and refining their arguments. On board was $13,000 worth of champagne.

John Brown captured the Federal arsenal in Harpers Ferry on October 16, 1859, without firing a shot. The next morning 2000 people, including a company of Washington Marines, charged the door, wounding Brown. He would be hanged for murder and treason on December 2, 1859.
(WESTERN RESERVE HISTORICAL SOCIETY)

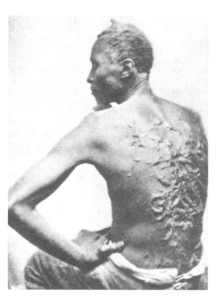

❧ THE FREEDOM FIGHTERS

Blacks in Canada had no problem choosing sides in the American Civil War. Enlisting in the Union cause in great numbers, they too fought for "life, liberty and the pursuit of happiness."

CONVINCED LONG BEFORE Lincoln's Emancipation Proclamation that the fight against slavery and the preservation of the Union were synonymous, Henry Jackson, a black Canadian, wrote: "I wish to impress upon your mind that the war is a trial between freedom and slavery not only here, but all over the world." True to his convictions, he enlisted in the Union Army and was killed at Campbell's Station on November 16, 1863.

Black Canadians had no problem in choosing sides in the American Civil War. Bred in slavery, they rallied to the Union cause as soon as President Abraham Lincoln issued a directive allowing black enlistments in the Union armies. Maritimers made their way to Massachusetts to enlist in the

RIGHT: *By 1860, one out of every seven Americans was a slave.* (U.S. ARMY MILITARY HISTORY INSTITUTE)

OPPOSITE PAGE: *A slave shows the signs of a severe whipping. Although one of the causes of the American Civil War's was Abolition, Abraham Lincoln did not issue his Emancipation Proclamation urging the release of slaves until the war's second year.* (JOHN JUDKYN MEMORIAL, BATH, ENGLAND)

famous 54th Regiment, celebrated in the movie *Glory*, while young blacks from the Elgin and Buxton Settlements in Ontario crossed the border at Detroit to join the 1st Michigan Coloured Infantry. Others, encouraged by Joseph Henson, a schoolteacher at Dresden whose escape from slavery inspired Harriet Beecher Stowe's book, *Uncle Tom's Cabin*, would serve in the cavalry, artillery and navy in every theatre of war. Two of every 100 Canadians who served were black Canadians fighting for the freedom of black Americans.

Although most black Canadians were American born, blacks had settled in Canada as early as 1629 when David Kirke arrived at Quebec with a black slave from Madagascar who he promptly sold to Champlain's master-builder, Guillaume Couillard. Little is known about this first black resident of Canada except that he was baptized under the name Olivier Le Jeune, served as a domestic and died, still a young man and a slave, in 1654.

Slavery was forbidden in France, but Louis XIV gave it limited approval in Canada, informing the colonists that "His Majesty finds it good that the inhabitants import Negroes there to take care of their agriculture." Blacks were soon set to work as household servants and field hands and did much of the heavy work in the new fur-trading outposts. Although there would be fewer slave-owners in New France than in the neighbouring English colonies to the south, the attitude to slavery was similar. Enumerated with the animals, a black was a slave everywhere and no one was astonished to find him in bondage.

Harriet Tubman (1820-1913), the most famous of the abolitionists, she helped thousands of Southern slaves escape to the northern U.S. and Canada through the Underground Railroad. Tubman also served for a time as a nurse in the Union army. (LIBRARY OF CONGRESS)

Slavery in Canada continued to flourish under the British regime, Jeffrey Amherst assuring the Marquis de Vaudreuil, a slave-owner, that "Negroes of both sexes shall remain in their quality of slaves in possession of the French or Canadians to whom they belong." This assurance was included in the Articles of Capitulation signed at Montreal in 1760.

Many prominent citizens acquired slaves. The Reverend David Delisle of the Church of England in Montreal bought a slave name Charles in 1766 and two years later James McGill, a wealthy merchant, bought "a Negro woman named Sarah, about the age of 25 years for the sum of 56 pounds, lawful money of the Province." Much of the dealing in slaves was carried on through the newspapers. When Fleury Mesplet founded the *Montreal Gazette* in 1778, he announced that his paper would "give notice to the public at any time of slaves deserted from their masters."

Slaves accompanied the Loyalists to their new homes in British North America in the wake of the American Revolution. Veterans of Butler's Rangers who settled along the Niagara Frontier brought slaves with them or bought them from livestock dealers who brought their wares to Canada. A Colonel Clark of Ernestown in Prince Edward County recalls that "drovers used to come in with horses, cattle, sheep and Negroes, for the use of the troops, forts, and settlers in Canada, and my father purchased his four Negroes, three males and one female named Sue."

Wherever the Loyalists brought their slaves, black settlements began to form – at Birchtown near Shelbourne in Nova Scotia; at York, Kingston, and Prescott; at Sandwich, Amherstburg and Chatham. Although they came as slaves, hope was beginning to dawn. In 1791, Colonel John Graves

After the Fugitive Slave Law was passed in the United States, the Underground Railroad led an estimated 40,000 blacks to Canada by 1861. And on August 1, 1894, Emancipation Day's 60th anniversary was celebrated in Amhertsburg, Ontario. (ONTARIO ARCHIVES)

Simcoe, the newly appointed governor of Upper Canada, pledged himself never to support any law that "discriminates by dishonest policy between the Natives of Africa, America or Europe." Two years later he introduced a bill in the Legislative Assembly prohibiting the importation of slaves, which passed "with much opposition but little argument."

In spite of its limitations, Simcoe's bill helped to change public attitudes to slavery and by the turn of the century most Canadian blacks were free. Moreover, American blacks, learning that they would not be enslaved north of the border, began a trek to freedom honouring Simcoe's memory with an abolitionist song:

> *I'm on my way to Canada*
> *That cold and distant land*
> *The dire effects of slavery*
> *I can no longer stand –*
> *Farewell, old master,*
> *Don't come after me.*
> *I'm on my way to Canada*
> *Where coloured men are free.*

The legendary Underground Railroad, with its mythical "trains" running through the northern states to terminals in Canada, had no track or rolling stock. It was underground only in the sense that it was a secret operation. Quakers and Methodists, free blacks and slaves, "shareholders" united in their hatred of slavery, worked out of border states and used railway terms to confuse the authorities. "Conductors" drove carts and farm wagons with slaves hidden in false compartments and transferred them to "stations" along the many routes leading to Canada. The most famous, Harriet Tubman, called the "Black Moses" of her people, made repeated trips into the South to guide slaves north. Her forays ended at St. Catharines at the home of the Reverend Hiram Wilson, the leader of the local refugee community. Operating informally without reports, meetings and memoranda, the Underground Railroad spirited some 30,000 fugitives to Canada between 1800 and 1860.

Harriet Tubman continued her work during Civil War as a spy and nurse for the Union Army. Discriminated against and denied a pension, her experience was only too familiar to Canadian black volunteers. Black soldiers did not receive the same pay as whites and could not become officers. Many served for long periods without pay until they were grudgingly awarded half the standard rate, prompting the 54th to adopt the bitter battle cry: "Three Cheers for Massachusetts and Seven Dollars a Month!" The men who died in the attack on Fort Wagner were never paid.

Military hospitals had separate but unequal facilities for black and white troops leading to a higher death rate among blacks. Only eight black surgeons received commissions and they were they were resented by their white colleagues. Dr. Alexander Augusta, who had trained at Trinity College in Toronto, was removed from his position as head of surgery at Camp Stanton in Maryland after his white assistants personally complained to the Secretary of War. Returning to Washington by train, he was attacked by two men who tore his officer's insignia from his uniform while a mob watched.

Approximately 180,000 blacks served in the Union Army. They participated in over 500 military engagements, 40 of which were major battles. Their most difficult battle, however, was waged against entrenched racial attitudes. American and Canadian blacks alike, faced the fires of war and hatred with courage hoping that they too would finally have the right to "life, liberty and the pursuit of happiness."

OPPOSITE PAGE: *This Fenian soldier is armed with a .58 calibre Springfield musket. His uniform is a green cavalry jacket from the Civil War period.* (PAINTING BY RON VOLSTAD, DND)

❧ THE FENIANS

The Fenians, a militant nationalist group, flourished among the Irish in the United States. Its agenda included the establishment of an Irish government in exile – in Canada.

"A FAERY SCENE!" an Irish immigrant wrote in the summer of 1846. "There are glades and groves, and wild flowers, and trees and shrubs that grow down to the water's edge and are mirrored in it so that the island seems to float." A few days later, he died of typhus and was buried in a mass grave in a wooded hollow. Nearby, a monument was later erected, and on its base is an inscription that reads: "In this secluded spot lie the mortal remains of 5294 persons, who flying from pestilence and famine and Ireland in the year 1846, found in America but a grave."

The place is Grosse-Île, a small, idyllic island in the St. Lawrence 30 miles downstream from Quebec City. For more than a century, it served as a quarantine station and as many as four million immigrants to Canada spent time there. At least 15,000 are buried beneath a Celtic cross that rises above a rocky promontory overlooking the river. During World War II and at the height of the Cold War the island also served as a top-secret site for the manufacture of anthrax and other biological weapons. It is a quiet, mysterious place, haunted by its history, which is slowly being transformed into a national park.

The Grosse-Île Quarantine Station was established in 1832 by the government of Lower Canada, alarmed at an outbreak of cholera in Europe. All vessels would be required to anchor at the station for inspection before being allowed to proceed to Quebec. Soldiers from the 32nd Regiment at the Citadel were sent down to the island to build quarters for doctors and nurses and long, narrow sheds with tiers of bunks to receive the sick. Within weeks, the island's fledgling facilities were swamped with desperately sick immigrants, and despite the medical staff's best efforts, cholera spread up the St. Lawrence and 3000 to 5000 died before the end of summer. Most were Irish.

Ireland, at mid-century, was a catastrophe waiting to happen. Over eight million people, roughly three times the present population, occupied the land; and on arable land, the population density exceeded China's. Land, largely controlled by absentee British landowners, was divided and subdivided again and again for the sake of increased rents until families were attempting to farm and live on less than half an acre.

The structure of Irish life had been produced by a single factor: potato cultivation. This was the situation in 1845, when an unknown disease attacked the crop and newly harvested potatoes melted into a slimy, decaying mass. During the next five years, one and a half million Irish were to die of starvation and another million were to be lost through emigration.

The poorest sailed as human ballast aboard timber ships – "Floating Coffins" – bound for Quebec. The voyage of the *Larch* out of Sligo in April 1847 was typical. Of 440 passengers, 106 died at sea and 150 arrived in Canada infected with typhus. By May, more than 40 ships stood off Grosse-Île in a line stretching several miles down the St. Lawrence. The dead lay in the holds among the living and were removed with grappling hooks. Hundreds of the sick were left on the beaches to crawl to dry land as best they could.

The fever-crazed roamed the island, died and were buried where they fell. Doctors and nurses, soldiers and volunteers, Catholic and Protestant clergy were overwhelmed by the tide of misery washing ashore. In that terrible summer, 37,000 Irish making their way to Canada died at sea or on our shores. The survivors, feared by the local population, made their way upstream into the interior by York boat or barge. In forest clearings, as navvies on the canals and later on the railways, as labourers and maids in the cities, they struggled to build new lives for themselves and their children.

But large numbers of the immigrants had no desire to resettle under the Union Jack. Most longed to go to the United States. By alleging that his intention was to settle in Canada, the prospective immigrant often procured free transport up the St. Lawrence, then simply walked across the border. "It is not well for those who are thinking of leaving their beloved homes in Ireland (wretched though they are) to think of Canada as a home," an Irishman wrote from Boston. "The employment which grows from enterprise which grows from freedom are not to be found there. It is a second edition of Ireland, with more room."

Thomas D'Arcy McGee, the most eloquent of the Fathers of Confederation, was an Irish Catholic editor and journalist who arrived in Boston in 1842. Two years later he was the editor of the Boston *Pilot* and became involved with Young Ireland, a group of nationalists who advocated rebellion against Britain. After ten years in the United States, however, he still felt like an exile and decided to move to Canada, a country whose "character is in the crucible." He had been to Canada before, speaking about ways to relieve the famine, including massive immigration to Canada, a scheme that the *Globe*'s George Brown condemned as "a movement to swamp the Protestantism of Canada by bringing into the province 800,000 unenlightened and bigoted Romanists." In 1857, McGee settled in Montreal and launched a nationalist newspaper, *New Era*. He was elected to the assembly the same year. "The one thing needed in Canada is to rub down all the sharp angles, and so remove these asperities which divide our people on questions of origin and religion," he wrote. "The man who says this cannot be done is a blockhead."

This was hardly the case in the United States, where the sharp angles of origin and religion defined the Irish, most of whom felt that they had been

With the possibility of an invasion stemming from the Fenians in the northern United States in the air, militiamen gathered in New Brunswick in preparation. (PUBLIC ARCHIVES OF CANADA)

driven from their native land by British injustice. Fraternal societies flourished, most dedicated to the overthrow of British rule in Ireland. They went by a variety of names: the United Irish Society, Corcoran's Irish Legion, O'Mahony's Guard, and the Phoenix Brigade. Some of them held regular parades and drilled from time to time. Although it is unlikely that more than 5000 men were involved in these societies at any given time, most Irish Americans were aware of their existence and approved of them. Drilling was a popular social pastime, and the idea that its ultimate purpose was the liberation of Ireland lent an air of romance to it all. Most of these societies posed no threat to anyone. The Fenians, however, were another matter.

Founded in Dublin on St. Patrick's Day 1858, the Irish Republican Brotherhood was dedicated to the aim of overthrowing British rule in Ireland and establishing a completely independent republic. It was more active in the United States, where its members were known as Fenians, a name derived from the Celtic "Fianna Eirionn," the ancient Irish tribal militia. The Fenians prospered, setting up headquarters in New York City and issuing bonds that merchants dealing with Irish Americans refused to purchase at their peril. Funds were readily subscribed and with hordes of soldiers of Irish origin recently discharged from the Union and Confederate armies, there was no lack of manpower. General T.W. Sweeney, a former Indian fighter who had lost his right arm in the Mexican War and who commanded

Thomas D'Arcy McGee (1825-1868), an Irish-born Canadian journalist, lived in the United States before moving to Montreal in 1857. The founder of the newspaper New Era, *he called for the federation of British North America, the building of a transcontinental railway, and the settlement of the west. He was elected to the legislative assembly of the province of Canada in 1858 and, after a brief time in the Reform Party of George Brown, joined the Great Coalition of Macdonald and Cartier. The most eloquent of the Fathers of Confederation, he noted that "had we not the strong arm of England over us, we would not have had a separate existence. He was elected to the House of Commons in 1867 and assassinated on April 6, 1868. (NAC)*

a division under Sherman in Georgia, was appointed secretary of war. "Fighting Tom," as he was known to the Fenian leadership, wasted no time gathering a staff and laying plans to invade Canada.

The Civil War was a vast battle school that educated a generation of Irish Americans, North and South, in the arts of war. Corcoran's Brigade, in which D'Arcy McGee's brother served, became one of the most famous corps in the Union army. It was virtually a Fenian force, as political propaganda was tolerated in Irish units as long as they were kept up to strength and fought well. Irish Americans in uniform provided a ready recruiting ground for Sweeney and the Fenians.

At the Fenians' fourth convention in Pittsburgh in February 1866, delegates met to discus the disastrous collapse of a recent uprising in Ireland. Embittered by this latest failure, a group of militants introduced Sweeney to the assembly. Sweeney then astonished those present by proposing an invasion of Canada. Theoretically, his plan, which called for the envelopment of the Canadas by a three-pronged attack along the border from Maine to Illinois, was feasible. While the left and centre wings would mount a diversion into Canada West to draw defenders away from Montreal, the right wing, which was nearly twice as large as the others combined, would strike from Vermont and New York State to cut the lines of communication and capture Montreal and Quebec City. An enclave in the Eastern Townships would be then be carved out and held as an Irish republic in exile.

Recruiting efforts were increased in the United States as well as in Canada, volunteers being promised bounties and grants of land. No one seems to have doubted for a moment that all would go well. The loquacious Sweeney told a Chicago audience: "We have strength, resources and opportunity beyond anything that has ever blessed the hopes of Irishmen before... Before the summer's sun kisses the hill tops of old Ireland, a territory will have been conquered on which the green flag, the sunburst of old Ireland, shall float in triumph, and a base be formed for some glorious operations."

In May 1866, the Fenians marched on Canada singing this ditty:

We are the Fenian Brotherhood, skilled in the arts of war,
And we're going to fight for Ireland, the land that we adore.
Many battles we have won, along with the boys in blue,
And we'll go and capture Canada, for we've nothing else to do.

The Sweeney plan, however, had a major flaw. It relied on support from the Irish in British North America – after the French the largest ethnic group in the emerging Dominion of Canada.

Fenian rhetoric did not escape the attention of the British and Canadian governments. British diplomats in the United States provided a steady stream of reports while the intelligence network set up by John A. Macdonald in 1864 to keep an eye on Confederate sympathizers shifted its focus to watching Fenians. D'Arcy McGee used every opportunity to speak out against them. "The Civil War has bred a clan of men averse to returning to the paths of peace," he told an audience of Irish Canadians in Toronto. "These fighting men wanted a cry, a cause, and a field of plunder. Do not flatter yourselves, however, that you have done with Fenianism. Either President Johnson must put it down in good earnest, with its ringleaders, or we ourselves must put it down in blood on Canadian soil. I need hardly add that my present politics for Canada are, plenty of breech-loaders for our volunteers and complete union amongst our people."

Macdonald called out the militia twice in response to Fenian threats – in November 1865 to garrison Prescott, Niagara, Windsor and Sarnia, and in March 1866 to guard the border in anticipation of a St. Patrick's Day invasion. The invasion did not materialize, but a month later the Fenians did strike – at Campobello Island in New Brunswick, burning a few buildings before the whole enterprise collapsed. The raid, however, was a blessing for

Macdonald as it marked a swing in public opinion in the Maritimes towards Confederation. In a subsequent election, corrupt even by the standards of the day, Leonard Tilley and the Confederationists were returned to power in New Brunswick, partly through fear of another invasion, and partly through bribes to the electorate.

The Fenians presented a more real threat in Canada West. Here, on June 1, 1886, they crossed the Niagara River and defeated a force of badly led Canadian militia at Ridgeway, a few miles from Fort Erie. Both sides suffered: about ten killed and as many wounded before the Fenians retreated to the United States.

At the same time, two other Fenian forces threatened Canada East from Vermont and New York State. Both raids amounted to little more than forays for food. After briefly flying the Fenian flag from Pigeon Hill, just inside the Canadian border, the raiders beat a hasty retreat and were promptly rounded up by U.S. troops.

The Fenians remained a threat for the next four years, staging another ill-fated raid at Eccles Hill in the Eastern Townships in June 1870. Confronted by Canadian militia and home guards, they withdrew with three dead and ten wounded.

The Fenian raids, which the U.S. government did little to stop, could hardly be considered an invasion. Still, the fact that the raiders, lacking both numbers and organization, could terrorize border towns from the Niagara River to the Bay of Fundy, was an indication of just how vulnerable the British North American provinces were. Confederation would mean a stronger and more efficient militia for home defence and a stronger voice in dealing with Washington.

D'Arcy McGee, had always been the most forceful critic of the Fenians, which made him unpopular with some Irish Catholics. In Ireland he had experienced the savagery of sectarian violence. "Secret societies are like what the farmers in Ireland used to say of Scotch grass," he wrote. "The only way to destroy it is to cut out by the roots and burn it into powder."

On the night of April 6, 1868, McGee left the House of Commons, lit a cigar, and walked to the boarding house on Sparks Street where he stayed while in Ottawa. He was looking forward to returning to Montreal to celebrate his birthday with his wife and family. As he was turning his key in the lock, he was shot in the back of the head and died almost immediately.

It was generally believed that his murder was the work of the Fenians. Patrick James Whelan, a young Irish immigrant, was arrested within 24 hours. He was tried and found guilty, although he maintained his innocence. Additionally, it was never proven that he was a Fenian. He was hanged before a large crowd in Ottawa – the last public hanging in Canada. McGee's funeral, held on what would have been his 43rd birthday, was the largest Montreal had ever seen.

BELOW: *Thomas D'Arcy McGee's funeral procession in Montreal.* (NAC)

OPPOSITE PAGE: *The Battle of Ridgeway, June 2, 1866. Taking place partly in the town of Fort Erie in southern Ontario (no stranger to battle after the numerous skirmishes of the War of 1812), the battle matched Fenian Civil War veterans from the United States against Canadian volunteers. It was the only major skirmish during the Fenian raids of 1866.* (ONTARIO ARCHIVES)

❧ THE BATTLE OF RIDGEWAY

Confusion, farce, and the fog of war enveloped the battlefield as the Canadian militia confronts the Fenians.

"THE FENIANS THIS MORNING invaded Canada," Amelia Harris wrote in her diary on June 1, 1866. "They crossed the river from Buffalo below Black Rock. It is telegraphed that there are 1500 of them. One thousand volunteers and some companies of the 16th have gone to repel them. It is to be hoped that we shall have a good account of them by tomorrow... The garrison had arranged for a picnic... but on account of the Fenians no one was allowed to leave the barracks, so the picnic was turned into a dance in the mess room. Edward, Sophia and George went."

Harris, who began to keep a diary in 1857 after she was widowed at the age of 52, lived in Eldon House, a gracious limestone manor overlooking the Thames River, near London. An acute if somewhat disapproving observer of the political and social life of Canada West, she described John A. Macdonald as "a clever man whose moral character I despise." Her diary reflected the daily concerns of the time, and in June 1866, her foremost concern was the Fenians.

Two days later, news that the Fenians were in Fort Erie reached Harris in church as militiamen in the congregation, she noted, left during the litany. The next morning, they and other militia units from across Canada West were routed by the Fenians at Ridgeway, leaving behind 10 killed and 38 wounded. Three others later died of exhaustion or sunstroke. "The Fenian excitement continues but not so absorbing as it was," Harris wrote on June 5. "There is a great feeling against General Napier and Colonel Peacock... It is said that Gen. Napier was drunk and that Col. Peacock delayed so that the volunteers were sacrificed."

By June 18, the volunteers had all returned to their homes, and Harris moved on to other things. "In the evening all of the Eldon party went to see the *Merchant of Venice* murdered," she wrote. "The performance was even worse than they expected."

The Battle of Ridgeway was hailed by the Fenians as the first Irish victory since Fontenoy in 1745, when the Irish Brigade of the French army overwhelmed the Coldstream Guards. In reality, it was a little more than a minor skirmish in a farmer's field.

Nevertheless, the man of the hour was General John O'Neill, the 32-year-old veteran of the U.S. army who led the attack. An able tactician who was appointed to his command just hours before the invasion was launched, his victory at Ridgeway propelled him to the top of the Fenian movement. Fenian folklore had it that he received no more than a few verbal instructions about his mission and did not even have a map of the country.

O'Neill arrived at Buffalo, New York, on May 30 and made his headquarters in Townshend Hall, where the Fenians held nightly meetings. A Canadian intelligence agent, John McLaughlin, reported that the city was full of "many strange military men," some wearing Union uniforms. Buffalo was the obvious base for an attack on Canada as it had large Irish population and several hundred Fenians wandering about would be more welcome here than elsewhere. When questioned, many said they were going west to seek work on the railways. Although an alarmed McLaughin informed Canadian authorities there were at least 1500 Fenians in Buffalo and more expected, his warnings of an immanent invasion went unheeded.

A mood of complacency seems to have set in after the Campobello fiasco.

McLaughlin shadowed the Fenians the night of the invasion as they moved down the Black River Road to board canal boats towed by tugs that took them across the Niagara River. McLaughlin estimated their strength at between 850 and 900 men. At 3:30 a.m. they stepped ashore at Frenchman's Corner, a mile south of Fort Erie and unfurled the green flag of the 17th Kentucky Regiment, which like all the flags carried by the Fenians bore a golden sunburst.

O'Neill's obvious objective was the Welland Canal, 13 miles west of where he landed. But until reinforcements arrived, he was content to occupy Fort Erie, cut the telegraph wires, and set fire to a railway bridge that linked the town with Port Colborne. His plans to seize wagons or railway rolling stock were frustrated by local residents who also drove their horses and livestock into the woods. By midmorning, his force was entrenched on Justice of the Peace Thomas Newbigging's farm, three miles north of Fort Erie. Security seemed rather lax as newspaper reporters from Buffalo freely visited the camp, along with the collector of customs at Fort Erie and Detective Charles Clarke.

In the meantime, McLaughlin's report set alarm bells ringing. Governor General Lord Monck called out 67 militia units, condemning the invaders as "a lawless and piratical band." Volunteers rushed to the colours, swelling the ranks of the militia to 20,000. The commander of all British and Canadian troops in Canada West was Major General George Napier. His immediate concern was to guard the Welland Canal and he acted accordingly, dispatching troops under the command of Lt.-Col. George Peacock to St. Catharines and Port Colborne, to secure both ends of the canal. Peacock was a steady, reliable officer, albeit without combat service. This lack of experience, and his plodding manner would have a major effect on the battle to come.

Peacock's troops were equally inexperienced. More than half of the militia recruits were under 20 and had never fired a shot. Maj. Charles Gillmor, who commanded the Queen's Own Rifles at Ridgeway, later testified that "they were as a rule partly drilled, some men undrilled." Their lack of experience was only matched by their enthusiasm. Private George Mackenzie of Hamilton's 13th Battalion recalled:

Fenians engage Canadians from behind the cover of trees and a split-rain fence. (PAINTING BY ALEXANDER VON ERICKSON, FORT ERIE MUSEUM BOARD)

"About 9 a.m. we formed fours and our march to the front began. In the meantime, an excited crowd had assembled outside the Drill Shed and the band of the 16th Regiment, British regulars, had come to play us down to the station. As we emerged upon the street the band struck up a lively air and a vast shout arose from the crowd. It was immensely thrilling. I felt as if I had risen to twice my ordinary stature."

The 13th arrived at Port Colborne late that night, having picked up the York and Caledonia rifle companies of the Haldimand county militia along the way. The Queen's Own Rifles were already there, cold, tired and hungry after a long journey from Toronto. As the senior officer present, Hamilton businessman Lt.-Col. George Booker found himself in command. Unfortunately, Booker had never commanded in the field before.

Meanwhile, the forces under Peacock's direct command were assembling at St. Catharines. After consulting a "dime map" provided by the post office, Peacock decided to move out and rendezvous with Booker at Stevensville, a small town near Ridgeway on the railway line between Port Colborne and Fort Erie. The ubiquitous Detective Clark informed him that the Fenians were encamped near Black Creek, numbering about 450, and drinking heavily. In fact, a very sober O'Neill had been informed of the Canadian presence by mounted scouts and had already made plans to intercept Booker's column before it could join forces with Peacock's.

Breaking camp at dawn, O'Neill deployed his men along the Lime Ridge Road, flanking a 30- to 40-foot high ridge between Stevensville and Ridgeway. Sending out pickets into the surrounding orchards and fields, he built a barricade out of rail fences and waited.

Militiamen stand near the body of a Fenian who was killed at the Battle of Eccles Hill on May 25, 1870. Casualties during the Fenian Raids were extremely light on both sides. Despite much bravado, when confronted by a determined foe, the Fenians showed little true conviction to their cause. They had, wrongly, been led to believe that disgruntled Canadians would rise up against the British and welcome the Fenians as liberators. (BROME COUNTY HISTORICAL SOCIETY)

Riding the 13th Battalion's only horse, Booker blissfully marched his 850 man force towards Ridgeway, with the Queen's Own Rifles leading. "We were a hungry, thirsty and depressed lot," a soldier recalled, "and we trudged along the road the road in silence for about an hour." Suddenly, the advance guard came under scattered fire from the Fenian pickets.

When firing began in earnest, Booker deployed the Queen's Own into line. Advancing in good order, they slowly pushed the Fenians back. Alexander Muir, the future composer of *The Maple Leaf Forever*, recalled that "we continued advancing for some distance, perhaps three hundred yards at a time, when the orders came for the Queen's Own to fall back on its supports. We had been under fire three quarters of an hour." Muir's sense of time was somewhat different from that of Major Skinner's of the 13th who claimed that "about ten minutes elapsed from the time the first shot was fired until some men of the Queen's Own came in and we were ordered to relieve the skirmishers. At the same time, Ensign Malcolm McEachren was carried to the rear." McEachren was the first Canadian killed in action.

The 13th advanced through the Queen's Own, driving the Fenian pickets out of the orchards and reaching the Lime Ridge Road. At this point, the tide of battle began to shift as Fenian resistance stiffened. Muir recalled that "I distinctly saw the enemy retreating a long distance before them towards a bush in the rear. Suddenly they seemed to rally and came down upon the line of the 13th, yelling. The Fenians advanced in a loose manner, but in great strength; then the 13th retreated at the double, but I did not hear the 'retire' sounded for that purpose."

With the Canadian line under pressure everywhere, Booker gave the Queen's Own the fatal order to form a square to repel cavalry. There was no cavalry, but panic set in and the Queen's Own broke and ran. Booker was unable to stop them.

"We ran forward fast, many of us being barefoot after the march of the night before, but they ran faster, a confused crowd of red and dark green, throwing away their muskets, knapsacks and overcoats," a Fenian recalled. "We pursued them for three miles, into the town of Ridgeway, and found the place deserted by all except one man. Their dead and wounded lay along the road and in the fields."

The Fenians did not have long to enjoy their victory. With scouts bringing in news of a force of British regulars approaching from Chippewa, O'Neill ordered a retreat to Fort Erie leaving ten dead, six seriously wounded, and 63 prisoners behind him. After a skirmish with a company of Welland militia, they re-occupied the old fort. O'Neill subsequently said: "Many of my men had not a mouthful to eat since Friday morning; and none of them had eaten anything since the night before, and all, after marching nearly forty miles and fighting two battles, they were completely worn out with hunger and fatigue."

That night, O'Neill and his men re-crossed the river and were promptly taken into custody. The American government, embarrassed by the actions of its Irish citizens, had had enough. The U.S. army and state militias were ordered to put a stop to "hostile expeditions." The Fenians would try again. In 1870, when O'Neill led another raid, and again in 1871, when no longer an officer of the Brotherhood, he led a small band of men in an attempt to liberate the "down-trodden people of Manitoba." This time he captured a trading post at Pembina – only to be arrested by a troop of American cavalry who had pursued him across the border.

The Fenians continued to hope and dream until the 1880s, when the movement faded away. After Ridgeway, its lasting contribution was Confederation.

OPPOSITE PAGE: *Snider rifles were used at the Battle of Ridgeway.* (DETAIL FROM PAINTING, ONTARIO ARCHIVES)

ಶ ARMING THE DOMINION

*The new Dominion's troops were armed
with a bewildering assortment of weapons
ranging from percussion muskets to
swords.*

THE FORCE THAT MET the Fenians at Ridgeway, was typical of
the pre-Confederation militia. It was short of ammunition, had no knapsacks, water bottles, blankets or cooking utensils and very little food. A
company of the Queen's Own Rifles had only 32 rounds of ammunition
per man for their Spencer rifles. The rest of the Regiment was armed with a
bewildering assortment of weapons ranging from percussion muskets to
Colt Navy revolvers and swords. The Welland Field Battery was issued with
Long Enfield Rifles because their field guns were unserviceable. The regulars carried the Brunswick rifle, one of the worst weapons of its time.

As a result of the Fenian raids, the governor general made an urgent
appeal to the British Government for a supply of Snider-Enfield rifles. The
Snider action had just been adopted for converting muzzle-loading Enfields

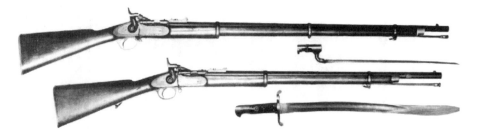

ABOVE: *Snider-Enfield rifle and carbine. Over 30,000 of these weapons were loaned to Canada in 1867 to equip the militia. They remained in service until 1900.*

to breech-loaders and was gradually coming into service in the British Army, replacing the hated Brunswicks. As a considerable delay was anticipated, several thousand single-shot Peabody rifles and Spencer repeaters were bought in the United States. Patented by Christopher M. Spencer, the seven-shot Spencer carbine and rifle had seen extensive use in the Civil War.

The first shipment of Snider-Enfields, 30,000 rifles complete with bayonets and accoutrements, arrived at Quebec in late 1867 as a loan which later became an outright gift. They were issued to infantry and rifle battalions, artillery units and the Grand Trunk Brigade. The Long Rifle was the principle weapon of the Canadian volunteer and permanent force until the mid-1890s and was not completely withdrawn from service until 1900. It saw service in the last Fenian Raid of 1870, the Red River Rebellion and the North-West Rebellion in 1885.

The British Army had adopted the Snider system in 1886 to convert their large stocks of percussion Enfield muzzle-loading rifles into breech-loaders. The Snider-Enfield was to be a stopgap weapon until a new breech-loading rifle could be developed. However, it proved to be very reliable and much better than most of the breech-loaders then available.

The action was screwed on to the Enfield barrel, which was shortened at the breech and chambered for a .577 cartridge. It took the form of a trough, level with the lower edge of the chamber. The cartridge was placed in the trough, pushed forward into the chamber, and the space was filled with a block, hinged from the right side, which contained a firing pin that was struck by an external hammer. After firing, the breech was opened and the block pulled towards the rear, which extracted the cartridge. The rifle was then turned over to eject the casing.

In 1874, 2100 Martini-Henry rifles were purchased in England, most of which were placed in storage in Montreal until 1885 when they were issued for use in the North-west Rebellion. Another 5000 were acquired the following year for infantry and rifle battalions while those supplied to the militia were turned in and the Snider-Enfield reissued.

As soon as the Snider breech had been adopted in 1886, the British government advertised a competition for a new rifle, to consist of an action and barrel capable of the same standard of accuracy found in the best muzzle-loading rifles. The trials that followed lasted until 1871 when the Martini action was fitted to the 33-inch Henry rifled barrel and officially adopted as the new service rifle.

The action consisted of a falling block hinged at the rear and operated by a lever located behind the trigger guard. A cartridge was fired by a striker driven forward by the action of a strong coil-spring within the breechblock. Lowering the lever ejected the cartridge casing. It was a good, single-shot rifle, which, unfortunately, could not be readily converted to a repeater.

The model 1876 Winchester lever-action was a larger version of the famous 1873 model, built to handle heavier calibre military cartridges. More than 64,000 were manufactured until the model was discontinued in 1867.

The rifle was operated by lowering and raising the lever to open the breech, extract the fired cartridge, feed a new one from a tubular magazine below the barrel, and close the breech. Military models were .45 - .75 calibre and were fitted with a heavy rear sight. It weighed eight pounds and held nine cartridges in the magazine.

The Winchester carbine with its 22-inch barrel was used by the Canadian militia and by the North-West Mounted Police and remained in service until well after the turn of the century.

In 1912, all military rifles in Canada, including the Lee-Enfield, were withdrawn from service. They were replaced by an infamous design based on the Model 1890 Austrian Mannlicher – the Ross Rifle.

FOLLOWING PAGE: *The Fathers of Confederation pose on the veranda of Government House, Charlottetown, Prince Edward Island, September 1864. (PAC/C-733)*

❧ CONFEDERATION

A "one-horse service," the new Dominion of Canada's permanent force was bedevilled by patronage and incompetent "jack-daw" officers parading in peacock's plumes.

THERE WERE PICNICS AND parades, fireworks and artillery salutes across the new Dominion of Canada on July 1, 1867, except in the Maritimes where the streets of Halifax were draped with black bunting. In Toronto, the Queen's Own Rifles, forgiven the fiasco at Ridgeway the year before, formed up with the 13th Hussars and 17th Foot on Denison's Common and went through their drill as little boys cheered and waved Union Jacks. Sir George-Étienne Cartier would proudly declare that "the Crown of Confederation is military force."

Sir John A. Macdonald had other ideas, however, as the public turned its attention to canals, railways and the settlement of the west. No provision was made to create even a small standing army and he would continue his pre-Confederation policy of acquiring defence on the cheap, relying on Britain and an ill-paid militia. "He looked upon money voted for militia purposes only as a means of gaining political ends," a critic noted. "But he was honest enough to keep the use of it within strict limits, and consequently cut down the estimates to the lowest possible level."

Nevertheless, the Militia flourished in the years immediately following Confederation. Forty-four new regiments were formed between 1868 and 1875, bringing the total to just over 70. The first Militia Act, adopted in 1868, created nine military districts and provided for an Active Militia of 40,000 volunteers, stiffened by half-pay British officers. In a class-conscious society, a Militia commission became a badge of place. Would-be officers were required to pay an entrance fee to city regiments, learn elaborate mess etiquette, and spend lavishly on uniforms. The wealthiest sponsored regimental social activities, sporting events and bands, which became the showpieces of the Militia's public image.

Summer camp became a common Canadian experience as thousands of citizen soldiers marched off each year to stage mock battles, drill and fire 30 rounds on the ranges with antiquated Snider-Enfield rifles. Training was simple and repetitive and totally inadequate. A colonel with the Haldiman Rifles complained that "the camps are a mere sham." The men are blarneyed or bribed for the occasion only. Half-grown boys or decrepit old men, if they can only hold a rifle, are accepted with thanks, and when the camp is over, the whole thing vanishes like snow off a ditch."

Whatever its limitations, the Militia was equal to its only real responsibility – aid to the civil power. Volunteers guarded a hanging in Toronto, broke up illegal boxing matches and cock fights, compelled farmers to pay taxes and were regularly called out to protect warring Catholics and Orangemen from each other and to put down illegal strikes. Relying on the Militia to maintain law and order had its drawbacks, however. When Grand Trunk railway workers went on strike in 1875 in Belleville, Ontario, for example, the local regiment, the 15th Argyle Light Infantry, could not be called out because most of its members worked for the railway and were already manning the picket lines. Moreover, employers regularly fired workers absent on strike duty or docked their pay.

In 1870, the militia was twice credited with saving Canada, turning back a Fenian invasion at Eccles Hill, Quebec and suppressing the First Riel Rebellion on the Red River. But, the Militia bloom began to fade and enlistments dropped off as the sense of urgency which had compelled men to join diminished. It soon became obvious that the Militia, poorly trained and equipped, was totally inadequate to meet Canada's defence needs.

The withdrawal of the British garrison from Quebec in November 1871, was a watershed in Canadian military history. For the first time, Canada was forced to assume responsibility for its own defence, disabused of the notion that it was an Imperial problem to be financed by the British taxpayer. Accordingly, two batteries of garrison artillery were formed to take over the fortifications at Kingston and Quebec and to act as schools of instruction for the Militia. Each was commanded by a British lieutenant-colonel assisted by eight Canadian officers who signed on for a minimum of three years.

Permanent commissions became available and the batteries flourished both as gunnery schools and the professional home of the Canadian artillery. In 1874, Major General Sir Edward Selby Smyth was appointed as the first General Officer Commanding (GOC) of the Militia, establishing an independent command structure, and $500,000 was appropriated to begin work on what would become the Royal Military College at Kingston. Prime Minister Alexander Mackenzie hailed these steps as "the foundation of a future national military system."

Sir John A. Macdonald, no friend of the regular military, returned to power in 1878 and immediately reverted to his old ways of rewarding political friends and associates with commissions in the militia. In 1883, seemingly acting out of character, he announced the formation of a 750-man Permanent Force. His motives became clear when it was revealed that all of the 21 officers appointed to the Infantry and Cavalry School Corps, nine of whom lacked military experience, were loyal Conservatives. Militia officers were not happy at the prospect of being taught by influential incompetents and the regulars themselves were frustrated when their own training was circumscribed so as not to offend the Militia.

Absurd as the situation was, Macdonald had managed to placate both the British and the military establishment. Canadians, preoccupied with the transcontinental railway and western settlement, hardly noticed. Only the *Ottawa Citizen* complained of "jack-daws in peacocks' plumes" parading in "a one-horse service."

That service was sorely tested during the course of the North-West Rebellion when supply, transport and medical services were found wanting. Ammunition was lacking despite the government's decision to set up a cartridge factory near Quebec and so many of the Militia's Snider rifles proved useless that an emergency order had to be placed in Britain for 10,000 Martini-Henries. Yet, the demands of patronage were met, even in time of crisis.

Patronage would bedevil the Permanent Force for the next 30 years. Able men who supported the wrong political party, or who lived in parts of the country already well represented in the army, were ignored, while political friends were rewarded with preferential treatment and accelerated promotion. There was no sense that officers or men needed to study their profession. Morale suffered and by the early 1890s, the desertion rate reached a staggering 17 per cent per year.

The pernicious effects of patronage even extended to the battlefield. Time and again, Colonel William Otter, commander of Canada's Boer War contingent, was forced to contend with subordinates as they jockeyed for position to replace him. Pandering to the system that had created them, Canadian officers routinely attempted to advance their careers at the expense of their comrades through direct appeals to friends in Parliament.

The *Canadian Military Gazette*, the self-proclaimed "Organ of the Canadian Army," regularly published diatribes against "political hacks and hangers-on" who found a career in the military without the least regard to "qualifications and merit." Publicity like this simply reinforced traditional Canadian antipathy to the standing army – a sentiment that is never far beneath the surface.

TIMELINE OF EVENTS 1764-1867

1775 Lexington and Concord ("Shot heard round the world"). Americans led by Montgomery take Montreal. Assault on Quebec unsuccessful. Washington organizes Continental Army.

1776 American troops retreat from Canada. British defeat Americans on Lake Champlain. Washington crosses the Delaware and is victorious at Battle of Trenton.

1777 Unsuccessful British plans to seize Hudson Valley. Battle of Brandywine (British victory). Battle of Saratoga (British surrender). Battles on the Mohawk.

1781 Privateering at its height as Maritime privateers harass American shipping. British surrender at Yorktown.

1792 – 1802 French Revolutionary Wars. Napoleon rises to power.

1794 Battle of Fallen Timbers (U.S.) Defeat of Indians helped bring Indian allies to British side in War of 1812.

1797 Battle of St. Vincent. Jervis and Nelson defeat Spanish fleet.

1798 Battle of The Nile. Nelson annihilates Napoleon's fleet.

1800 Battle of Marengo. Napoleon defeats Austrians.

1803 – 1815 Napoleonic wars engulf the Continental.

1805 Battle of Trafalgar. Nelson defeats French and Spanish fleets. Austerlitz – Napoleon victorious over Austrians and Russians.

1808 – 1814 Peninsular Campaign Wellington ties down the French in Spain and Portugal.

1812 Napoleon defeated in Russia

1812 – 1815 War of 1812.

November 7, 1811 William Henry Harrison attacks Tecumseh's village on the Tippecanoe in an attempt to expand Indiana Territory.

June 19, 1812 War declared. Fueled by Tippecanoe and the Royal Navy's impressment of seamen from U.S. vessels, war was encouraged by American desire for expansionism by "War Hawk" party. Poorly-planned U.S. invasion of Canada aborted.

July 17, 1812 British capture Fort Michilimackinac.

August 16, 1812 Brock captures Detroit without loss against vastly superior American force.

August 19, 1812 *USS Constitution* destroys *HMS Guerrière* off Nova Scotia.

October 13, 1812 Battle of Queenston Heights. American invasion attempt fails. Brock is killed.

November 19, 1812 Americans at Rouses Point, New York. Militia refuse to cross border and return to their winter quarters.

January 22, 1813 Major-General Harrison musters troops to retake Detroit but is defeated by the British at Frenchtown.

April 17, 1813 American troops under General Henry Dearborn capture York (Toronto). They withdraw on 8 May after a powder magazine explodes.

May 27, 1813 Winfield Scott captures Fort George for Americans. British garrison withdraws from Fort Erie.

May 28 - 29, 1813 British assault on Sackets Harbor fails.

June 1, 1813 HMS Shannon defeats USS Chesapeake off Boston Harbour.

June 6, 1813 British win battle of Stoney Creek, Ontario, and reoccupy Fort Erie. Dearborn retreats to Niagara.

September 10, 1813 Commodore Perry defeats British fleet and establishes U.S. navy mastery on Lake Erie.

September 29, 1813 Detroit recaptured by Americans.

October 5, 1813 Battle of the Thames at Moraviantown. Harrison's troops defeat British. Tecumseh is killed.

October 25, 1813 Battle of Châteauguay. Voltigeurs and militia turn back larger American invasion force, then return to their winter quarters.

November 11, 1813 American General Wilkinson, advancing east on Montreal, is defeated at Crysler's Farm, and retreats.

December 18, 1813 British capture Fort Niagara.

December 29, 1813 British column burns Buffalo and its navy yard.

March 30, 1814 U.S. offensive repulsed at Lacolle Mill. General Wilkinson relieved of command.

July 2, 1814 U.S. troops cross Niagara River, seize Fort Erie for the second time.

July 5, 1814 Battle of Chippawa. American victory. (West Pointers wear grey to commemorate first use of this colour by American troops.)

July 25, 1814 Battle of Lundy's Lane. Bloody five-hour battle ends in a draw.

August 31, 1814 North-East Maine occupied and annexed to New Brunswick.

September 11, 1814 Battle of Plattsburg. British naval force defeated. Sir George Prevost withdraws from much smaller American land force.

September 17, 1814 Americans sortie from Fort Erie; over 1000 casualties in resulting battle. Fort Erie later abandoned. Final major action in north.

December 24, 1814 Treaty of Ghent ends war and is ratified on 11 February 1815. Pre-war boundaries restored.

January 8, 1815 Andrew Jackson becomes a national hero when his rag-tag army defeats General Pakenham at the Battle of New Orleans, 15 days after the Treaty of Ghent was signed.

1816 Seven Oaks Massacre. Métis and Selkirk settlers clash at junction of Red and Assiniboine Rivers in what is now central Winnipeg. One Métis and 20 settlers are killed.

1837 Unrest in Lower Canada. Louis-Joseph Papineau's revolt is violently suppressed by British troops.

1837 Rebellion in Upper Canada. William Lyon Mackenzie stages an unsuccessful revolt in Toronto.

1838 Battle of the Windmill. American incursion is turned back by the militia.

1839 Lord Durham submits his report recommending the union of the Canadas.

1854 – 1856 Crimean War. Britain, France and Turkey ally against Russia.

1854 Battle of Balaclava. Canada's first VC is earned during the Charge of the Light Brigade.

1857 – 1858 Indian Mutiny. Canada's second and third VC's are awarded.

1861 – 1865 Canadians participate in the American Civil War (see separate headings).

1862 Garibaldi invades Italy's Papal States. Canadian volunteers serve in "Papal Zouaves."

1864 Charlottetown Conference. Confederation of British North American colonies is discussed.

1866 – 1870 Fenian Raids

July 1, 1867 Dominion of Canada comes into being. Sir John A. Macdonald sworn in as Prime Minister.

Index

**Read about Canada's military and
its rich history… *Every month!***

Esprit de Corps, Canada's
only independent military
magazine, chronicles the
current and historical exploits
of the Canadian Forces. An
award-winning combination of
investigative journalism and
informative military history...
Subscribe today!

***For more information, call
1-800-361-2791 or
www.espritdecorps.ca***